How to Use Feedback Marking in the Classroom: The Complete Guide

By Mike Gershon

Text Copyright © 2017 Mike Gershon

All Rights Reserved

About the Author

Mike Gershon is an expert educationalist who works throughout the UK and abroad helping teachers to develop their practice. His knowledge of teaching and learning is rooted in the practicalities of the classroom and his online teaching tools have been viewed and downloaded more than 3.5 million times, making them some of the most popular of all time.

He is the author of over 80 books and guides covering different areas of teaching and learning. Some of Mike's bestsellers include books on assessment for learning, questioning, differentiation and outstanding teaching, as well as Growth Mindsets. You can train online with Mike, from anywhere in the world, at www.tes.com/institute/cpd-courses-teachers.

You can also find out more at www.mikegershon.com and www.gershongrowthmindsets.com, including about Mike's inspirational in-school training and student workshops.

Training and Consultancy

Mike offers a range of training and consultancy services covering all areas of teaching and learning, raising achievement and classroom practice. He runs inspiring and engaging INSET in primary schools, secondary schools and colleges. Examples of recent training events include:

- Growth Mindsets: Theory and Practice – William Bellamy Primary School, Dagenham
- Creating a Challenge Culture: Stretch and Challenge Reimagined – Manchester College
- Rethinking Differentiation – The British School of Brussels

To find out more, visit www.mikegershon.com or www.gershongrowthmindsets.com or get in touch via mike@mikegershon.com

Other Works from the Same Author

Available to buy now:

How to Develop Growth Mindsets in the Classroom: The Complete Guide

How to use Differentiation in the Classroom: The Complete Guide

How to use Assessment for Learning in the Classroom: The Complete Guide

How to use Bloom's Taxonomy in the Classroom: The Complete Guide

How to use Questioning in the Classroom: The Complete Guide

How to use Discussion in the Classroom: The Complete Guide

How to Manage Behaviour in the Classroom: The Complete Guide

How to Teach EAL Students in the Classroom: The Complete Guide

How to be an Outstanding Trainee Teacher: The Complete Guide

More Secondary Starters and Plenaries

Secondary Starters and Plenaries: History

Teach Now! History: Becoming a Great History Teacher

The Growth Mindset Pocketbook (with Professor Barry Hymer)

The Exams, Tests and Revision Pocketbook

Also available to buy now, the entire 'Quick 50' Series:

50 Quick Ways to Get Past 'I Don't Know'

50 Quick Ways to Start Your Lesson with a Bang!

50 Quick Ways to Improve Literacy Across the Curriculum

50 Quick Ways to Improve Feedback and Marking

50 Quick Ways to Use Scaffolding and Modelling

50 Quick Ways to Stretch and Challenge More-Able Students

50 Quick Ways to Create Independent Learners

50 Quick Ways to go from Good to Outstanding

50 Quick Ways to Support Less-Able Learners

50 Quick and Brilliant Teaching Ideas

50 Quick and Brilliant Teaching Techniques

50 Quick and Easy Lesson Activities

50 Quick Ways to Help Your Students Secure A and B Grades at GCSE

50 Quick Ways to Help Your Students Think, Learn, and Use Their Brains Brilliantly

50 Quick Ways to Motivate and Engage Your Students

50 Quick Ways to Outstanding Teaching

50 Quick Ways to Perfect Behaviour Management

50 Quick and Brilliant Teaching Games

50 Quick and Easy Ways Leaders Can Prepare for Ofsted

50 Quick and Easy Ways to Outstanding Group Work

50 Quick and Easy Ways to Prepare for Ofsted

Series Introduction

The 'How to...' series developed out of Mike's desire to share great classroom practice with teachers around the world. He wanted to put together a collection of books which would help professionals no matter what age group or subject they were teaching.

Each volume focuses on a different element of classroom practice and each is overflowing with brilliant, practical strategies, techniques and activities – all of which are clearly explained and ready-to-use. In most cases, the ideas can be applied immediately, helping teachers not only to teach better but to save time as well.

All of the books have been designed to help teachers. Each one goes out of its way to make educators' lives easier and their lessons even more engaging, inspiring and successful then they already are.

In addition, the whole series is written from the perspective of a working teacher. It takes account of the realities of the classroom, blending theoretical insight with a consistently practical focus.

The 'How to...' series is great teaching made easy.

Acknowledgements

My thanks to all the staff and students I have worked with past and present, particularly those at Pimlico Academy and King Edward VI School, Bury St Edmunds. Thanks also to the teachers and teaching assistants who have attended my training sessions and who always offer great insights into what works in the classroom.

Contents

Chapter One – Why Feedback and Marking Matter 11

Chapter Two – Effective Feedback 27

Chapter Three – Efficient and Effective Marking 43

Chapter Four – Verbal Feedback 59

Chapter Five – Written Feedback 75

Chapter Six – Targets and Target Implementation 91

Chapter Seven – Further Feedback Techniques 107

Chapter Eight – Further Marking Techniques 123

Chapter Nine – Exemplar Questions 137

Chapter Ten – Exemplar Targets 149

Chapter Eleven – Conclusion and Select Bibliography 167

Chapter One – Why Feedback and Marking Matter

What is Feedback?

Feedback is at the heart of this book, just as it needs to be at the heart of the learning process. It is through feedback that students gain access to the information they need to progress, learn and develop. Feedback is the means through which teachers communicate their expertise to students, bridging the gap between minds. In the teacher's mind there is a wealth of knowledge, understanding and expertise. In the learner's mind there is less of this. Feedback is one of the ways the teacher transfers expertise from their own mind to the learner's mind. The success of this transfer is generally greater if the learner has opportunities to use, think about and act on the feedback they receive.

Feedback shapes student effort. It is expert information provided by the teacher which the learner would struggle to access independently. Through feedback, the teacher helps students target their efforts, improve their thinking and change the processes in which they engage.

Students can provide themselves with feedback – and many do. For example, a learner may attempt a task, look at the results, compare these to what they wanted and make changes. Or, a learner might find a question challenging and so go off and read an article about the topic to develop their understanding. But in this book our focus is on teacher feedback, and the things teachers can do through their feedback and marking to support students and help them to be successful.

That is what we will explore. The purpose is not to deny the efficacy or existence of student feedback. Instead, it is to focus on the things teachers can do to maximise their own impact. And, implicit in this, there is an understanding that teachers provide feedback which students might struggle to access on their own. To illustrate the point, think about a class you teach. If left to their own devices, how many would find ways of giving themselves feedback and what level of quality would that feedback reach? Now, compare this to the expert feedback you could provide in a single lesson, or by marking a set of books. The difference is significant.

Thought of in this way, we can see why feedback is such a central feature of teaching. It is the means through which the teacher coaches their learners. It is distinct from the role of conveying content, though closely related. After all, if students are not learning about something or how to do something, it is much harder to give them feedback. Feedback needs a subject. It must be on something.

Let us take a step back for a moment, though, and consider how feedback works on a wider scale.

Imagine you arrive home after a long day at work. Winter is on its way and the temperature has dropped. Immediately on entering the house you turn on the central heating. Slowly, the house begins to warm. After an hour or so, the heating switches itself off. Why? Because you have a thermostat. This measures the temperature in a given room and clicks off when that temperature reaches or exceeds the temperature you have set. So the house gets as warm as you want, but no warmer.

Now consider what happens when your thermostat is broken. The house may get warmer and warmer, with the central heating only turning off when you physically intervene. Or, it may never warm up, unless you go to the boiler and manually override the settings.

With a thermostat driven heating system, feedback is at work. That feedback is of a rudimentary kind. It is the heat in the room in which the thermostat is placed. The thermostat reads this through a temperature sensor and responds accordingly.

This, in wider terms, is how we can define feedback. Information from the environment communicating a sense of what is going on.

Feedback in the classroom shares some elements of this definition but necessarily goes further.

When we use feedback as part of our teaching, we give students information about what is going on with their learning. Traditionally, this information concerns what they are doing well and what they could do to improve. Here we see a special feature of classroom-based feedback. It tends to be directional. That means, it tends to tell students something about what is happening but, in so doing, also conveys a message about how what is going on can be changed, developed or improved.

This differs from feedback as found in our thermostat central heating system. There, the feedback has more of a brute function – to flip a switch. To change the state of the heating system from on to off, or vice versa.

In the classroom, feedback serves the teacher's wider purpose, the one which animates all their work: helping students to learn. Feedback is used as a way to support learning. Ideally, it should be used as a way to maximise learning; to help students make better progress, think more deeply and learn more than would otherwise be the case.

To best understand the impact of effective feedback, let us imagine what learning would be like without it.

Learning Without Feedback

Many of us learn without feedback. At the moment I am reading a book about a topic with which I have little familiarity. Through reading the book I am learning. No teacher is required; no teacher feedback is given.

I'm sure you will have learned many things in your life independently, without anyone else's intervention. Indeed, if you are reading this book at the moment, on your own, as is likely to be the case, then you are learning without feedback. There is no teacher on hand giving you information to direct your efforts or to improve the way in which you are thinking about the text.

If feedback is not necessary for learning, then why is it deemed so important? Why did you decide to buy this book to find out more about it? And why do various major meta-analyses of educational research (see for example Black et al 2003; Hattie 2008; Higgins, Kokotsaki and Coe 2012) consistently place feedback at the top of the pile when it comes to effective teaching and learning interventions?

We can think about the answers to these questions by visiting a classroom in which no feedback is given. One in which the teacher does not provide any student with any information about what they are doing well, what they are doing not so well and how they could improve.

In this classroom, the teacher arrives, teaches the lesson and then leaves. They mark student work but do not give any feedback other than, perhaps, summative responses in the form of marks, levels or grades. But maybe they don't even provide this.

So where do learners find themselves? First, their interactions with the teacher are severely restricted. A large proportion of the feedback we give is verbal. If feedback is excluded from our imaginary classroom, then the teacher is not interacting with students in anything like the way we would normally do. Second, there is great ambiguity for students over where they are at and where they are going. They are left to work out for themselves if what they are doing is right. And they will have to give themselves targets or goals if they want something to pursue. Third, the teacher's expertise remains locked in their head. Students have no access to it. They cannot take it and make it part of their own thinking. Nor can they use it to direct their efforts.

In short, a huge amount is missing. The classroom is a sparser place. So much of the richness is lost. Content is being conveyed, yes. But beyond that there is little else.

Now compare this classroom with another – one I'm sure is more familiar.

In our second classroom the teacher arrives, teaches the lesson and then leaves. But during the course of the lesson they circulate through the class, talking to students, giving them feedback, making suggestions, modelling, scaffolding and asking questions. Maybe they also stop the lesson at a couple of points and give feedback to the whole class, re-teaching key ideas which are proving difficult for everybody to grasp.

When we look in student books we see formative marking. That is, marking in which students receive information about what they have done well and what they could do to improve. Finally, the teacher provides time in which students can work on their targets. During this time they call a few students up to the front of the class – students they've identified in advance – and work intensively with these learners, helping them to understand their most recent feedback, what it means and how to put it into practice.

There is so much more here than in our first classroom. Interactions are richer, more detailed and more closely connected to the learning in which students are engaged. The teacher actively looks for opportunities to deliver feedback – to transfer expertise from their mind to the minds of their students. And marking is used to help students understand what good looks like and to provide clear direction on where and how they should target their efforts in the future.

This is a far richer experience. One which makes better use of the teacher's skills, knowledge, understanding and expertise. One in which we would expect students to make better progress. While the evidence base tells us that feedback is effective, we can also deduce the fact through a thought experiment such as this.

As a final point, consider the journey a student goes through from the age of 5 to 18. In an ideal world, as they progress through the education system, so they are taught by individuals who are increasingly expert in specific subjects. A primary school teacher has to be expert in a number of areas, including some highly specific topics. But their expertise is necessarily restricted and they take on a more generalist role. A teacher of A Level, on the other hand, is expected to have a high level of expertise in one particular subject; and will probably have a particular specialism within that as well.

As the child moves through the system, so the feedback to which they are exposed becomes increasingly specialist in nature. The expertise they are accessing through teacher feedback when they are 11 is different from that which they access when they are 17. Again, though, imagine a child who goes from 5 to 18 and never receives feedback; who never has access to any expertise. For them, learning will usually be much harder, and probably less fulfilling as well. And so we see why feedback has the potential to have such an impact.

Assessment for Learning

Feedback and marking are intimately bound up with assessment for learning (AfL). However, I have written a separate book on this topic – How to Use Assessment for Learning in the Classroom: The Complete Guide – and do not want to repeat myself here. I also think it is important to focus on feedback and marking separately because of the central role they play in teaching and learning for most of us. As a result, I will attend only briefly to assessment for learning, connecting it to the points made thus far, before moving away from it. With that said, you can rest assured that everything contained in this book fits with the principles of AfL, and you might choose to read this book and the other book side by side.

Assessment for learning is the name given to a suite of strategies, activities and techniques in which formative assessment is the central feature. Formative assessment sees the teacher giving students information about their learning. They can use this information to understand what good looks like and what they need to do to improve. It differs from summative assessment in which learning is summed up and the relative success of the assessment is expressed through a grade, mark or level.

We can think of assessment for learning as three things:

- Eliciting and using information

- Giving formative feedback

- Opening up success criteria

Some may quibble with this formulation, but I stand by it as a sound rule of thumb for any teacher to use. It is developed from the original research and can be thought of as a cycle. The teacher elicits information about student learning and uses this to shape their lessons and provide feedback. They then open up success criteria and give students opportunities to implement their feedback. Having done this, the teacher is in a position to elicit new information, which they use to inform future planning and future feedback. And so the cycle continues.

Thought of in this way, AfL becomes a process of continuous improvement and development. It places the teacher in a coaching role. And it underpins the whole process of teaching and learning.

In terms of feedback and marking, we see the central role both play in the AfL cycle. Feedback is obviously one of the key components – you might even say the driving force. Marking is one of the most important ways through which teachers elicit information about student learning, information they can use to tailor their feedback so it is as effective as possible. Without access to information about student learning, it is much harder for a teacher to provide timely and useful feedback (though it is acknowledged that marking is not the only way information can be elicited).

You will note that these points tally with what we have said previously about the importance, relevance and efficacy of feedback. You will also note that there are some aspects of AfL I have put to one side for the purposes of this book – opening up success criteria being the main one (although do remember that feedback does this implicitly by indicating what is good, what is not so good and what could be improved). So we will leave it there, with the caveats that the other book is available and that the practical strategies, activities and techniques we look at in Chapters Two to Ten are focussed on feedback and marking but, by virtue of this, may also be thought of as part of assessment for learning.

Unlocking Your Expertise

Let us now return to one of the points I have been making throughout this introduction. We must look a little deeper at this idea of expertise and the notion that feedback is in large part a process through which you give students access to your expertise; through which you unlock your expertise so they can take it, use it and make it a part of themselves. So they can learn from it.

The argument goes like this. In the classroom we are not all equal when it comes to knowledge and understanding. The teacher is the expert. That's why they are there. That is why they have to be qualified to do their job. And that is why they are in charge of planning and delivering lessons.

These are obvious points yet often overlooked. Many teachers equate the desire for equality in the classroom with the idea that we are equal in all areas.

This is a misrepresentation of the truth. Equality in the classroom concerns the notion that all students have an equal right to learn, to be treated with respect and to be seen as individuals. Few, if any, could argue with that. But it does not mean that the teacher is the same as the students. They aren't. They are there precisely because they are not the same. This difference is the characteristic necessity of their being the teacher.

Students may teach each other at times, may offer peer mentoring, may engage in peer-assessment (and all three of these activities are efficacious) but they do not and cannot take on the role of teacher full time. To suggest they can (and that, therefore, they are equal to the teacher in all matters) is wrong.

The teacher is the expert. Their expertise covers the curriculum they teach, but it also covers their wider cultural knowledge, their understanding of teaching and learning, their knowledge of psychology as it relates to the classroom and their knowledge of the students they work with.

All of this expertise is what separates the teacher from their students, and which puts them in a position to teach and to teach well. A teacher who fully understands the curriculum, who has a broad cultural understanding, knows teaching and learning inside out, has an intimate understanding of psychology in the classroom and who knows their students really well is in an incredibly strong position from which to teach effectively. And this will encompass giving good feedback on a regular basis.

When we give students feedback, we give them information about what they are doing and what they could be doing. We elicit information about their learning, perhaps through marking but also through observation, questioning and listening, and we then provide feedback based on what we have elicited. This means we make a judgement. Something along the lines of: What do I now know about this student's learning, and therefore what useful information can I give to help them improve?

We rarely articulate this but it is a fair representation of the process underpinning our behaviour. In answering the question – in providing relevant feedback – we make reference to our own expertise and then deliver information to students based on this, in a form they can understand and will be able to use.

For example, a maths teacher uses their expertise in maths to give feedback which is relevant, meaningful and useful. They may also use their expert knowledge of their students to tailor this feedback so it is well received. And they might call on their expert knowledge of the curriculum to make a link between what they are asking students to try next and how this will help them further down the line.

For me, seeing feedback as being about unlocking your expertise has much to recommend it. First, it reminds you that you are an expert and that your expertise is valuable; you can use it to shape and direct student effort. Second, it suggests that the wider role of teaching is to bring students closer and closer to your level of expertise, even to help them surpass it. This is neatly summed up in the old quote: 'The student becomes the master.' Why do they become the master? Because the master's expertise is no longer superior to their own. They are equivalent, or the student's has surpassed the master's.

Third, it gives you a rule of thumb you can turn to whenever you are delivering feedback – be that written or verbal. You can always ask yourself the question: how can I make sure this feedback gives the learner access to my expertise? In asking this question you direct your own thinking towards the area of your expertise which is most relevant to the matter in hand and you also remind yourself that your job is to translate that expertise so the learner can understand it and make use of it.

That, as I see it, is the essence of effective feedback.

Eliciting Information

Eliciting information is an essential part of giving good feedback. Without an accurate understanding of where your learners are at, it becomes far harder to provide feedback which is relevant to them. As noted, we elicit information in a number of ways: through observation, by listening, by asking questions and by marking student work. In this book our focus is on feedback and marking and so we will look mainly at the role of marking in the elicitation of information, while also noting that this is the primary mode of delivery for written feedback. With that said, at no point do I intend to suggest that other methods of eliciting information should be rejected. Far from it.

A really effective teacher will probably see all interactions with their students as opportunities to elicit information. They will use signs and signals in the classroom to modify their teaching, their lessons, and their behaviour, as well as the feedback they give.

For example, an effective Year 6 teacher may carefully observe the way in which different learners respond to an increase in the level of challenge after lunch. Knowing their students well, they will modify what they have planned in light of what they see and hear. Similarly, an effective A Level PE teacher may carefully observe how different students engage with a set of warm-up drills, using the information they elicit to modify the individual tasks and targets they set for those students in the next part of the lesson.

These examples illustrate the role eliciting information plays in the AfL cycle. Returning our focus to feedback and marking, we can say that a teacher who is in full control of the feedback they give – who is on top of it and is using it in a manner which suits them and their students – will almost always be eliciting the information necessary for making successful judgements.

For example, they may plan assessments with the express intention of revealing information that will be useful to them. This sounds obvious, but how many assessments are planned simply as a way to close off a topic? A carefully planned assessment sees the teacher creating a task, series of tasks or set of questions which allow them to elicit the information they deem most useful. They do this in full knowledge that the information is what they want to get their hands on; that it is this which will allow them to give the best quality feedback.

A common example of good practice here is hinge questioning. This is a short, in-lesson assessment method in which the teacher poses a question on which the learning hinges. If students get the question right, and can back up their answers, they can move on. If they get things wrong, or are uncertain, then this signals to the teacher that further action is required. When planning a hinge question, the teacher first identifies the key piece of learning on which everything hinges, then develops a question which will elicit both correct answers and incorrect answers. Getting mistakes and misconceptions into the open is as important as getting the correct answers out.

Only if the teacher is aware who is labouring under misconceptions and making mistakes can they intervene to remedy this – often by providing feedback.

Good feedback rests on accurate information about student learning. This principle is central to the book. It is another rule of thumb you can use to make decisions during your planning, teaching and assessing. It is also worth keeping at the forefront of your mind when you are marking. If you are not gaining access to the information you want, then that is an issue. It could be that you need to change the structure of your tasks, or that students are not fully engaging with the work.

Once you have identified the cause – whatever it is – you are in a position to do something about it. And, by making positive changes, you will elicit better information. The information you want. This, in turn, means you can give better feedback. Feedback more closely tailored to your learners' needs.

Sustaining Purpose and Targeting Effort

Feedback is an incredibly effective way to sustain student purpose and target learners' efforts. Let us return to our two imaginary classrooms from earlier. One in which no feedback is given, the other in which feedback plays a central role.

In the first classroom, the teacher makes no attempt to help students target their effort beyond setting tasks and delivering content. They may offer overarching explanations of why working hard matters, why the topic of study matters and so on, but this is not supported by personalised interventions or specific goal-setting in the form of targets. Some learners are relatively OK with this, particularly those who are self-motivated. But even these learners are losing out, because the teacher's expertise is not used to help them better sustain their purpose and target their effort.

While fostering independence is important, this cannot be to the exclusion of the most powerful tool at the teacher's disposal.

Let us now turn to the second classroom. In this one, we find that all students have a target and that the teacher gives them time to work towards this. We also see the teacher circulating through the course of the lesson, delivering feedback intended to support students and develop their learning. In this classroom, the teacher is using feedback to influence what students do and think: where they target their efforts, what they think is important, whether or not they are motivated.

A good example here is the comparison between a student who has a target and a student who doesn't have one. Imagine we are in an A Level Sociology classroom – somewhere of which I have personal experience. Student A has the following target: 'You need to bring more evaluation into the main body of your essay. Having described a key theory or piece of research relevant to the question, make sure you then critique this. Highlight its strengths, weaknesses and limitations. Don't be afraid to contrast theories or to use one piece of research to criticise another.'

Student B has no target.

What then happens, in terms of purpose and effort, when they come to write their next essay?

Student A has useful information from the teacher in the form of feedback. They can use this to direct their effort, safe in the knowledge that successful implementation of their target will lead to improvements. They also have a goal to aim at. And goal-directed behaviour tends to be a feature of sustained motivation. In addition, feedback of this type can cultivate a sense of intrinsic motivation. Students come to realise that they are in control of developing themselves and growing their own abilities (in growth mindset terms, they come to focus on learning goals, which are internal, rather than performance goals, which are external).

Student B does not have useful information from the teacher. They don't have any feedback. They may still perform to a high standard. And they may be able to sustain a sense of purpose and target their efforts effectively. This is particularly true of self-motivated learners, those who actively seek out success criteria, and conscientious learners. But we cannot be sure. And many learners in this position will find it much harder to effectively target their efforts compared to if they had feedback showing them how to do this. An absence of feedback, for many students, means an absence of direction. Or, at least, a harder path to finding direction.

This again emphasises the way in which feedback draws the teacher into a coaching role. We are giving students information they can use to change, modify and adapt what they are doing and how they are thinking. This is very much like the role of a coach. Unlike a coach, we also focus on delivering knowledge and cultivating understanding more widely – something a coach may do, but which isn't central to their job in the way that it is for a teacher.

So feedback is a powerful tool in part because it shapes the magnitude and direction of student effort, and helps to create and sustain a sense of purpose. Motivation being central to effective learning, after all.

One explanation I would suggest as to why the research indicates that feedback has such a big impact is because consistently receiving high-quality feedback (access to the teacher's expertise) means learners are consistently able to target their efforts in the most efficacious direction. While this is a perfect world explanation (we've all come up against those difficult situations when students ignore our feedback or refuse to see it in a positive light!) I still believe it has a lot to commend it; as demonstrated through the contrasting examples above and as, I'm sure, you could attest from receiving good, bad and indifferent feedback during your own learning experiences.

Raising Achievement and the Rest of the Book

Good feedback tends to lead to good progress. A lack of feedback does not augur well for raising achievement. As teachers, we are trying to do the best for our students. Feedback means we can give them access to our expertise. This makes it easier for them to target their effort and make progress. It also helps them to think and do things differently than would otherwise be the case. Through feedback we correct, coach and cajole students. We also support them, challenge them and give them access to opportunities which might otherwise pass them by – or not even come into their frame of reference.

We know from the research mentioned above that feedback can play a significant role in raising achievement. I have sought to demonstrate why this is the case through the course of this introduction. I would now like to add one final example to further support the argument, and to give you something to think about. Then I will briefly outline the remainder of the book – the practical chapters to follow.

You decide you want to learn a new language. Instead of going to one of the online courses available, you opt for a tutor. Someone who can give you face-to-face support. You have a look at the local listings and identify someone who sounds good. They say they speak Italian and that is the language you have chosen to learn. So you get in touch with them and put a date in the diary for your first lesson.

Because you are an experienced, mature learner you do some preparatory work using a combination of books, apps and the internet. You want to impress your tutor in the first session! And you want to convey a sense of yourself – what kind of learner you will be and your keenness to work hard in order to be successful.

On arriving at the first session, your tutor greets you warmly. The two of you sit down and begin to chat. 'Have you lived in Italy?' you ask them. 'No,' comes the reply.

'Is your family Italian?' you ask. 'No,' they say.

'Oh,' you reply. 'Did you study Italian at university?' The tutor shakes their head.

'A Level?' 'No.'

'Right. OK. Um, do you know Italian?'

The tutor smiles. 'Yes, of course. I took an online course last year and am well ahead of the novice stage. Now come on, let's get started!'

Why would this be a deflating experience for most people? Why would many people decide not to go back to the tutor after the first session but to find someone else instead?

Expertise. We want an expert. Someone who is at least reasonably more expert than us. This is because we want access to their expertise. And we want their feedback. Because it is that feedback which we know will help us to learn more quickly and more effectively. That will help us to target our effort and sustain our purpose. So we leave the early-stage, self-taught tutor after a single session and find someone whose expertise is well in advance of our own. And we do so because we know that the learning experience which follows will likely be much better (only likely because feedback and expertise are not the sole criteria of success).

So that is my message to you in this book. Be the expert. Give students access to your expertise. Do this by providing verbal and written feedback. Ensure students have time to act on and implement your feedback. And use every opportunity, including marking, to elicit information you can use to inform your feedback. That's where we're going; that's what the practical strategies will focus on.

Here is a list of the remaining chapters, along with a short summary of what to expect in each. You can read the chapters in order, or pick and choose – whatever works for you:

Chapter Two – Effective Feedback:

Describes and exemplifies some key principles you can follow to keep your feedback effective.

Chapter Three – Efficient and Effective Marking:

Does the same for marking. Also includes strategies to make marking efficient and save you time.

Chapter Four – Verbal Feedback:

Practical strategies and techniques you can use to make verbal feedback effective.

Chapter Five – Written Feedback:

Practical strategies and techniques you can use to maximise the impact of your written feedback.

Chapter Six – Targets and Target Implementation

Looks at target setting and how you can ensure targets are successfully implemented.

Chapter Seven – Further Feedback Techniques

A selection of additional techniques not included elsewhere, all focussed on feedback.

Chapter Eight – Further Marking Techniques

A selection of additional techniques not included elsewhere, all focussed on marking.

Chapter Nine – Exemplar Questions

Question-based feedback is explained and then exemplified through 150 exemplar questions divided into ten categories.

Chapter Ten – Exemplar Targets

150 exemplar targets, divided into the same set of categories.

Chapter Eleven – Conclusion and Select Bibliography

Sums up the book as a whole and provides a select bibliography for further reading.

Chapter Two – Effective Feedback

Introduction

We are now in a position to think about some of the features of effective feedback. In this chapter we will look at the following:

- Personalisation

- Clarity and Intelligibility

- Credibility and Relevance

- Manageability

- Scaffolding and Modelling Feedback

- Target Implementation and Active Practice

- Learner Agency

The list is not definitive but does, I would suggest, encompass the areas of greatest importance. As we look at each in turn, bear in mind that I am not suggesting all feedback should cover every feature. In some cases this might not even be possible. What I am arguing is that each of these features is something to aim for in your practice; a marker of high-quality feedback. That is, feedback which conveys useful information to the student, rooted in the teacher's expertise. Information which helps them to understand what good looks like, pushes their thinking, shows them how to improve and so forth.

In this chapter I will not make the distinction between written and verbal feedback. This is for two reasons. First, Chapters Four and Five deal with these separately. Second, it would make the explanation of ideas and practical strategies somewhat cumbersome. I feel confident in doing this because I know that you will be able to look critically at what I present and make your own judgements about how it relates to written and verbal feedback, based on your own experiences.

Finally, let me point out that if you are seeking to change the way in which you give feedback, or the nature of the feedback you give, it is good to begin by accepting that such a process can take a little while. Forming new habits takes time and making alterations to a core aspect of what you do on a daily basis won't happen overnight. Persistence, practice and trial and error are essential.

Personalisation

The first feature to consider is personalisation. Personalised feedback is feedback which is specific to the learner. This does not mean that it will always differ from the feedback other learners receive. For example, it is perfectly possible for two or more students to receive the same feedback from their teacher because they need to work on improving the same thing. However, the personalisation comes from the fact that the information delivered by the teacher is relevant to the learner who receives it.

Feedback which is not personalised may well not relate to the learner who receives it. Or, it might be clear to the learner that this feedback has come from another source, as opposed to any engagement with their work or learning. For example, we can imagine a teacher bringing out a sheet of feedback they use every year when teaching a given topic, handing it to their learners and saying something like: 'This is what I always tell students when we do this.'

Feedback of this type is disconnected from the learner's present experience. In our example, the teacher is relying on feedback they have formulated in years gone by. This may well remain relevant – but it is presented as a historical document from which learners are to make selections, as opposed to a response in the present to what learners are currently doing.

As part of a wider process of giving feedback, such a sheet may be useful. One example of this is when the teacher presents students with a mistakes crib sheet at the start of a topic, so they know what common mistakes have previously been made, and can then spot these in their own work should they arise. However, in this situation we can imagine the teacher continuing to give feedback during the topic, and relating this directly to the learning in which students are engaged.

Two questions you can ask yourself to ensure feedback is personalised are:

- Does this feedback relate to the information I'm eliciting or have elicited about students' current learning?

- Does the learner know that this feedback is for them and relates to their learning?

A simple technique through which to signal the personal nature of feedback is to attach the student's name to it:

'Paul, this is a really interesting answer. What I'd like to see is whether you can include as much detail in your next piece of work. Try to focus on that when you begin.'

Through this, the student sees the teacher treating them as an individual. This, combined with the signal that the feedback is specifically relevant to them, tends to be motivational.

If we now consider the logic underpinning the process of personalisation, we can note that feedback which is personalised is more likely to contain a high level of relevance for the student in question. This is because the teacher has elicited information about that student's learning and used this information to tailor a response based on their own expertise. Thought of in this way, we can see how personalisation is intimately bound up with a sound understanding on the teacher's part of where students are at, what they know, and where they need to go next.

It is not always possible to give personalised feedback to every student. Time does not allow it. In some cases, then, we might find ourselves delivering feedback to a group, or perhaps the class as a whole. In these situations it is good to emphasise that while this feedback is not being given directly to individual students, it is still a result of you having analysed what students are doing and what they need to change, improve or do differently (as well as what they are getting right).

For example, we might mark a set of student books and note that the class splits roughly into five groups, each of which needs to work on a specific area. We could then share this information with the class at the start of the next lesson and display five targets on the board, one for each group. After explaining that this feedback is personalised – because it is a direct response to what we have observed in student books – we could then circulate and offer further support as students identify the target appropriate to them and try to implement this.

In conclusion, personalised feedback motivates students by signalling that you are paying close attention to them and their learning. It is also more likely to be good feedback because the personalisation is a result of you having elicited accurate information about student learning.

Clarity and Intelligibility

Students have to interpret the feedback we give. They need to make sense of it. If they can't, then it becomes very difficult for them to use it. Opaque or unintelligible feedback is stripped of its usefulness.

When it comes to clarity, one of the best approaches is to consider the extent to which your feedback can be decoded by a student without any further support. This may mean rehearsing feedback in your head first, before you say or write it. The process of editing and refining means you are conveying an end product rather than an initial formulation. It need not take a long – a few seconds is usually enough.

In some cases, it is helpful to enhance intelligibility through examples. You can provide students with a brief demonstration of what the feedback means, refer them to exemplar work or ask them to compare their work with a partner's to identify similarities and differences. Extending this idea, you might choose to begin your lesson by exemplifying for the class as a whole some of the specific feedback you have given, so that everybody has an opportunity to access meaning.

A maths teacher, for example, might start their lesson by going through three key pieces of feedback they delivered to roughly seventy-five percent of the class. They would exemplify and talk through each one, taking questions from students as they went.

This points us to a wider issue. Once you have given feedback to your students, it is incumbent on you to be certain they understand it. If you don't make an effort to find out, there is the risk that your feedback will not have the desired impact. And you will probably only discover this further down the line, compounding the problem.

Here are some examples of techniques you can use to ensure clarity and intelligibility or remedy a lack thereof:

- Ask students to signal if they don't understand your feedback. Give them a sense of agency and encourage them to communicate with you as early as possible.

- After handing out books you have marked, circulate through the room and check learners understand their feedback.

- When giving verbal feedback, ask learners to repeat it back to you or to explain what it means.

- Scaffold and model some or all of the feedback you give (for more on which, see below).

- Tailor your feedback to the student in question. Bear in mind the language skills and level of subject knowledge they possess.

- Use examples, contrasts, diagrams and analogies to exemplify meaning.

- Stick to a structure for your feedback. For example, strengths first, followed by a target.

- If setting a task in which target implementation is central, plan to have a few minutes at the beginning during which students review their targets and can ask you for help if anything is uncertain.

- Use reflection and review to give students an opportunity to think about, discuss and analyse the feedback they receive. This may only be a couple of minutes, but it is time in which uncertainties will become apparent – giving you a chance to act.

- Identify specific students who struggle to interpret feedback. Make a point of working one-to-one with these learners to support their efforts.

To sum up, there are two strands to ensuring clarity and intelligibility. First, pay attention to how you formulate your feedback. Second, look carefully at how students respond, elicit information about their responses and be ready to offer further support where necessary.

Credibility and Relevance

In some cases, we may deliver personalised, clear, intelligible feedback yet still find ourselves in difficulties. Students either ignore our feedback or simply don't believe in it. In the latter case, this can lead to a half-hearted attempt to act on it, with disappointing results. In the student's eyes these results confirm their initial decision not to believe in the feedback.

Credibility and relevance are more often than not wrapped up with student perceptions. If a student perceives feedback as credible, if they perceive it as relevant, then they are more likely to be positively disposed towards it and to believe that acting on it can bring about positive change.

So what stops some students seeing feedback as either credible or relevant?

One of the most important factors is the learner's sense of self, as it relates to learning, or to the specific subject you are teaching. A student who does not believe they can get better at something will generally find it harder to believe that a piece of feedback telling them they can is true.

Imagine a student who does not believe they can better at art. Someone who believes artistic ability is innate and thinks they weren't born with the genes necessary to be artistic. This learner's sense of self in relation to art is antithetical to the underlying principle of feedback – the principle animating this book: that feedback is expert information provided by the teacher which learners can use to improve what they do.

Every time their art teacher gives them feedback, both the feedback itself and the underlying principle are butting up against the learner's beliefs about themselves and about what constitutes artistic ability. This conflict leads to the feedback losing credibility in the student's eyes. It's as if they are being asked to believe something (that they can get better) which runs contrary to a central belief they hold about themselves (I'm not artistic and therefore cannot improve).

Clearly this also impacts on the perceived relevance of the feedback. If the student is operating under a belief that they cannot change their abilities, then feedback of any type becomes largely irrelevant. One of the common ways in which this perception manifests itself is when a student refuses to put any effort into implementing a target, despite the teacher offering support, cajoling and coaxing the student to try.

Here, we see the student exercising a passive power (the ability to withdraw or not to act) in response to a belief that what the teacher thinks – and what their feedback implies – is untrue, and therefore not relevant to them.

When it comes to credibility and relevance, achieving our goal of delivering effective feedback is slightly tougher than in the other categories. This is because we are usually concerned with changing how students think about themselves, which takes longer and requires more sustained effort than making changes to our own practice and the things over which we have direct control. Such as the form our feedback takes and how we plan for students to interact with it.

Nonetheless, lots of options are open to us, many of which take their cue from work on growth mindsets, wherein the beliefs learners have about themselves and their ability to change, learn and develop take centre stage. Here are five techniques you can call on to change students' perceptions and therefore change how they view the credibility and relevance of the feedback you give:

- Acknowledge learners' beliefs, but then ask them to try anyway. This means we are not denying the learner's point of view but that we are asking them to put it to one side once it has been acknowledged. The technique doesn't always work, but sometimes it can be enough for a student just to know their voice has been heard.

- Use case studies which demonstrate how individuals have benefitted from feedback – how feedback has helped them to learn and to grow. You can use examples of famous people, former students, or current pupils and staff in school – including yourself. Case studies are easy to identify with because of the human interest and narrative structure. They are also an effective way to embody abstract ideas in concrete terms.

- Find two pieces of student work which demonstrate progress over time. This may or may not be a result of feedback you've provided. It is nearly always possible to find two appropriate pieces for any student. If you can't, think creatively. For example, you could compare how they spoke in class three months ago with how they speak now. Use the contrast between the two pieces of work to demonstrate the student's inherent capacity to improve and develop. Tie this to the benefits acting on feedback can bring and suggest that the student might like to change their mind in light of the evidence.

- Break your feedback down into a series of small steps. This can make life easier for a student who struggles to believe they have the ability to change. Smaller steps are easier to visualise than larger ones. They are also simpler to implement. Doing this is therefore about giving students an easier path through which to start acting on feedback, lessening the sense of risk (which is generally a by-product of fear of failure).

- Ask a student to give you feedback and agree that you will act on this if they act on yours. This calls on the notion of reciprocity and forms a social contract between you and the student. It can be risky and you will need to set the boundaries of what student feedback should entail. It is also good to stress that the student's feedback should take a similar form to yours – rational, specific and supported by evidence. If you can get all this in place, though, it can be a powerful experience for the student, binding them into the idea that feedback is both positive and non-threatening.

Overall then, issues of credibility and relevance are often tied up with student perceptions. Finding strategies through which to change how students think will help to dispel many of these.

Manageability

If you have seven targets to implement at the same time, good luck to you! If you have one on which to focus all your energies, I'll wager that you'll make short work of it.

Manageability is an important aspect of effective feedback. Deliver too much information to learners and they will struggle. Excess information tends to come in one of three forms. First, there can be too much information in total. Second, there is too much analysis of problems. Third, there are too many targets for students to work on. Here are examples illustrating each type:

1) The teacher provides extensive written feedback covering every aspect of the student's work. This is not broken down into sections but is delivered in continuous prose. It covers strengths, weaknesses and targets but these are not separated into different parts. It takes the student a long time to read what has been written and their immediate energies are spent synthesising the information and trying to identify which bits are most important.

2) The student receives a piece of work covered in red ink. To the extent that the original text looks like it is drowning. The teacher has gone through every sentence in meticulous detail. The annotations are legion. Each one is relevant, precise and based on the teacher's extensive expertise. But there is just too much for the student to process. By the time they have read through the first third of what the teacher has written they feel overloaded. They push the work to one side and convince themselves they will return to look at it later. Probably, they won't.

3) It's a practical lesson and the design and technology teacher is talking to a learner about their project. The teacher is an expert. They know everything there is to know about this project – about what works, what doesn't, what good looks like and what causes problems to arise. They try to share as much of their expertise as possible and end up giving the student eight different things to work on. By the time they move on to talk to another learner they feel pleased that they have successfully given access to their expertise. The original student, however, is completely

overwhelmed. So they just go back to doing what they were doing before the teacher arrived.

Notice how in each example there is no question about the teacher's intentions. They are good in all cases. The problems arise when the teacher's good intentions take over, to the detriment of manageability. Excessive information ends up negating the very thing it was meant to give rise to: development of student understanding and ability.

In the first example, the teacher is keen to make sure the student has a full understanding of everything they've observed about their work. But this is too much for the student to deal with. They don't need all of this information to be successful. They don't need all of it to develop or improve what they're doing.

In the second example, there can be little doubt that every annotation the teacher has made is correct – that it represents an accurate, unadulterated analysis of the student's work. But the student is not yet an expert, so there is too much here for them to process. Too much to get their head round. They don't have the range of prior knowledge and understanding the teacher possesses. They need the teacher to do some of the synthesis for them.

In the third example, the teacher delivers information that is relevant to the task and which, if followed, would no doubt lead to a highly successful project. But there is too much of it. The student is already juggling the different aspects of the task in their mind, at the same time as they are trying to bring their project in line with what they initially envisaged. The student does not have enough spare mental resources to process and act on the vast range of targets the teacher provides.

When it comes to manageability, then, less is generally more. It is important to consider when formulating your feedback, be it written or verbal, how easy it will be for the student to manage. Ask yourself whether they will be overloaded by what you convey. Ask yourself if you can break your feedback up or structure it in such a way that students can attend to different parts in turn. Consider how you would cope if given an excess of information to interpret and work on. Think about what else your students are trying to do in lessons, in addition to decoding and acting on your feedback. Finally, bear in mind that working memory is limited and that having to divide this between various targets seriously diminishes the likelihood of success.

Scaffolding and Modelling Feedback

Scaffolding and modelling are two of the key tools all teachers call on to help students understand ideas and information, successfully complete tasks, and make good progress. Scaffolding is the process by which you support students to learn and do more than they could manage on their own. It is the help you provide, tailored to their current circumstances. A good rule of thumb here is to give the least amount of help first. This means you promote independence and a sense of agency and don't fall into the trap of doing the work for the student.

Modelling can be considered as a type of scaffolding, though it is sufficiently important to warrant a distinction. It is the process by which we demonstrate ideas, processes and activities for students, helping them to understand these and giving them a model from which they can borrow, imitate or copy. This includes things such as modelling of thinking, modelling of skills and modelling of how to tackle a particular task.

When it comes to effective feedback, we can use scaffolding and modelling to help students understand:

- What their feedback means

- How to act on their feedback

- What implementation of their feedback will look like (what good looks like in this context)

- Where the feedback comes from and why it has been given

- How to tell if they have successfully implemented their feedback

This sees us using scaffolding and modelling in the same way as we would use it in any other area of our teaching, only with the subject of our endeavours being feedback, as opposed to anything else.

Our aim is to use scaffolding and modelling as ways to enhance the effectiveness of our feedback. For this reason, we will need to decide when it is appropriate and when it is unnecessary. For example, we might decide that some students will require regular scaffolding of their feedback because, for whatever reason, they struggle to deal with it on their own. On the other hand, we might identify some learners who will rarely require any support of this type, except on the odd occasion.

Here are five examples of how you can use scaffolding to make your feedback more effective:

- Turn a target into a series of three sub-questions. Indicate to students that by answering each question in turn they will achieve their target.

- Re-explain feedback to students who don't understand. Use simpler language and shorter sentences to increase clarity.

- Use concrete examples to contextualise abstract ideas. For example, if you have asked a student to be more critical, exemplify this through concrete examples of critical thinking.

- Break a target into two parts. Explain the different parts to a learner and ask them to focus on one at a time.

- Instead of writing feedback in continuous prose, deliver a series of succinct bullet point. For example, three strengths and one target. Then, offer further verbal explanation when students receive their feedback.

And here are five examples of how you can use modelling:

- Talk students through how you would go about trying to implement the feedback you've given. Model your thinking for them.

- Model the thinking which preceded your formulation of the feedback. This helps students to understand where the feedback came from and why it matters.

- Use exemplar work as a model which shows students what they are aiming towards.

- Sit down with students and model how to begin acting on their feedback. For example, if you have asked them to rewrite a section of their work, sit down with them and model the first part of this process, then invite them to take over.

- Model positive responses to feedback. Show students how to put emotional reactions to one side and see feedback in a positive light.

Target Implementation and Active Practice

If a student does not have the opportunity to act on the feedback they have been given, it is highly likely that the feedback will disappear into the ether, never to be seen again. Time moves on quickly in the classroom. And we soon find ourselves focussing on new content, new tasks and new ideas. Feedback becomes effective when time is provided in which students can act on it. While this is not a constituent of the feedback itself, it is an important supplement to the provision of feedback.

In Chapter Six we look at target implementation in detail, so I won't labour the point here. But there are a couple of things to say before we move on.

Active practice differs from passive practice. In the former students are actively attending to what they are doing. They are engaged in the process, meaning it has greater impact and requires higher levels of effort. For example, consider the difference between a child who is actively practising playing the piano and one who is passively practising. The former is engaged with their practice. They are thinking about what is happening and targeting their effort in pursuit of a goal: improvement. The latter is not engaged. They may be thinking about other things. They are going through the motions. As a result, they will probably not draw the same benefits from their practice nor make the same progress as their peer.

When it comes to target implementation, then, the first step is to provide time in which students can focus on using their targets. On putting them into practice. When it comes to active practice, we are aiming to set up situations in which students not only have opportunities to work on their targets, but find themselves fully focussed and engaged while they do.

Over a period of time, a student who is given repeated chances to implement targets and actively practice the necessary steps involved is far more likely to make enhanced progress than a student who receives feedback but is not given time in which to act on it, or who is given time but then remains passive and simply goes through the motions.

While more detail is given in Chapter Six, here are five relevant techniques to get you started:

- Make target implementation time a part of your planning. Just as you would plan starters, activities and plenaries, so too plan time in which working on targets is the primary focus.

- Use mid-lesson reviews to help students reflect on whether or not they are fully focussed on their targets.

- Plan lessons which lead on from written feedback. For example, if you've given your class feedback on their most recent essays, plan a follow-up lesson in which essay writing is the focus. This means students can immediately act on their feedback.

- Plan a series of short, sharp activities, one after the other, each of which gives students a chance to apply their feedback. For example, a PE teacher might plan five passing drills, each five minutes in length, to run consecutively. Learners are expected to focus on their targets in each successive drill.

- Highlight the difference between active practice and passive practice. Make sure learners understand how they differ and ask them to monitor their own efforts.

Learner Agency

The final feature of effective feedback I want to touch on is learner agency. This theme has come into view a number of times already. For example, when we looked at student perceptions, when we considered the manageability of feedback and when we thought about personalisation.

Promoting learner agency means promoting a sense that learners are in control of their learning and that they are the ultimate arbiters of their own success. Their views and actions have a significant influence on how feedback is received, how it is used and the extent of its impact.

If a student believes they have a degree of control over the process of receiving and using feedback, then they are, in most cases, more likely to see feedback in a positive light and to feel engaged with it. Compare this to a student who feels they have no agency. Feedback is done to them, rather than provided for them and developed with them. This is a very different place to be in, psychologically.

Personally, I would find it far less motivating – and less fulfilling as well. I imagine you would feel the same. Consider, for example, what it feels like if you are observed and then given feedback on your performance without any opportunity for discussion or comeback. And are then told you must implement whatever targets you have been given, regardless of whether you agree. Otherwise there may be consequences.

Being a professional and an adult you will probably put emotion to one side and get on with things for the sake of it (while also looking for another job!). But there'll still be a bitter taste in the mouth and a sense that something isn't quite right; that a better way is possible.

This same principle applies to learners. If we can help them to understand their own role in the provision and use of feedback, of the central part they play in determining their own success, then our feedback will tend to prove more effective. Equally, if we can create a culture in which students feel feedback is a positive thing, can see that it involves the teacher giving access to their expertise so the learner can use this to make changes, improvements and take control their own destiny, then good results will follow.

Ultimately, learner agency is about showing students they have choices in the classroom, that the choices they make influence what happens and that you, the teacher, are not there to make their choices for them, but to guide them in making good choices which have positive benefits for their current selves and their future selves. Following the principles of effective feedback as detailed in this chapter will take you a long way towards achieving this goal.

Chapter Three – Efficient and Effective Marking

Introduction – Why Mark?

We've already touched on this, so let's draw some of our existing thoughts together and supplement them with a few more.

Elicitation of information has to be one of, if not the, most important reason for marking. While the term can sound overly technical it is intended as a catch-all referring to the wider process in which the teacher engages when assessing student learning. Marking allows us to elicit information about knowledge, understanding, existing ability, skill levels, progress and so forth. The structure of the work we ask students to do plays a role here, as this determines, to some extent, what we find ourselves marking. Therefore, the scope of possible information we can elicit is at least partially circumscribed.

Put simply, we elicit different information from an essay and a poem, from video footage of a dance routine and a written explanation of how the routine was choreographed. This is not a problem. It just means we need to be aware that when we mark there may be information which we cannot access because of the tasks we have set. For this reason, it is good to think carefully in advance about what you want to mark and to consider using a range of assessment types.

Elicitation of information does not just include that which pertains directly to the curriculum. When we mark student work we also look at the processes they have used to produce their work, the level of effort they have put in and attendant factors such as how they have responded to challenges and whether their work suggests an interest and engagement with the topic. The point is that marking gives access to a broad range of information, not just a narrow one, and that this encompasses both curriculum matters and wider elements.

This takes us to the second key purpose of marking, to give feedback. And, as we have already seen, effective feedback rests on elicitation of useful information. By and large, we mark students' work and then return it to them. In lessons, we find ourselves assessing what students are doing in the present and giving them feedback in response, but there is a subtle difference. For the moment, let us stick to the traditional experience of marking.

We set the class some work, take in the books, read through and mark them and, in so doing, provide feedback. Some of this might be cursory or summative in nature – ticks, crosses, grades, marks and levels – some will highlight simple errors – underlining misspelt words, for example – and some will be of the type we are mostly concerned with in this book: formative feedback.

Whatever feedback we use – and it is often a combination of the above three categories – we do not make it a fundamental part of our marking while expecting that students will ignore it. Quite the opposite. We do it because we understand that it is an important mode of communication between teacher and student. To return to the idea outlined in Chapter One, it is a means through which the teacher can give students access to their expertise.

Marking is thus about improving our own understanding of where students are at and then turning this understanding around and using it to help students better understand where they are at, where they need to go next, what they need to change, keep the same, think about further, correct and so on. This is true for a tick or cross in the same way as it is true for a written target. The difference is in the informational content of those two forms of communication.

A cross indicates that the answer to which it refers is incorrect. Expanding this out, we can say that a cross signifies a discrepancy between the answer-ideal and the student's answer. I say 'answer-ideal' because a cross could be used to indicate incorrectness in an answer for which many possible correct forms could be given, just as it can be used to signal the same thing when there is only one right answer. In the first case, we might have a written response to a question, in the second case an answer to a sum.

When the student sees the cross, they understand what this is signalling, in the same way that they understand what a tick signals. However, they do not at this point have access to additional information which can help them to understand why the answer is wrong. This isn't necessarily a bad thing. In some cases it is exactly what we are after; because we want students to go back and work things out for themselves, or because we want them to think more carefully about work they assumed was correct.

Marking which is only ever of this kind does leave students short, though. The deficit can be characterised as a lack of more detailed information; a lack of access to the teacher's expertise. That is why formative feedback is so important, why it retains such power to help students develop, and why it is central to any explanation of why we mark.

So elicitation of information and provision of feedback in all its forms, but especially of the formative type, are the central reasons why we mark. But before we move on, it is worth noting a few supplementary explanations.

Marking can aid motivation. If students see their work is not being marked, they may start to question why they are bothering to produce it. Marking signals that you are attentive to the work students are doing and that you have their interests at heart. This doesn't mean you need to mark everything, all the time. But it does suggest that keeping up to date is important for maintaining morale as much as anything else.

A related point is that marking is a major means through which teachers can praise students. And praise is something from which we all benefit. It is an acknowledgement of ourselves as individuals, can be seen as a validation of things we've done, and also acts as positive reinforcement for the things which attract the praise. With that said, indiscriminate praise – praise which doesn't connect to specific things students have done – isn't necessarily to be recommend.

Learners will often see through praise of this type and view it sceptically. Or, they may come to assume that indiscriminate praise is the norm and that therefore they do not need to try, because praise will be forthcoming anyway; this being a simple function of them being who they are rather than a result of the things they've done and the effort they've exerted. Ideally, praise will not be trait focussed (you're brilliant) and will instead signal to students why what they've done is good (I love the way you kept going even though it was really challenging).

On a different note, marking allows us to fix feedback in time and space. This is in contrast to the ephemeral nature of verbal feedback. A number of benefits accrue. First, both we and our students can return to the feedback over time, meaning we can make comparative judgements. Second, we can be certain about what the feedback was. This is not always the case with verbal feedback. Memory lacks the permanence of marks physically inscribed on a piece of paper. Third, written feedback may be easier for some students to manipulate. For example, a learner may find it easier to reflect on a piece of feedback which is written down in front of them, as they do not need to hold this in their working memory while they reflect. The same cannot be said for verbal feedback.

The final reason I will mention is tracking progress over time. This connects to our earlier point about eliciting information. As a teacher, we need to track progress over time so that we have a clear idea of where students are going, what progress they are making in summative terms and what sort of patterns and trends are visible for groups and the class as a whole. Regular marking enables this. And we may do it mainly for our own benefit, with students seeing the impact only tangentially through the changes we make to lessons and the interventions we put in place in light of what the data tells us.

Purposeful Marking

Having set the scene for why marking matters and, in so doing, indicated at least part of what effective marking ought to entail, let us now move on to think about efficacy and efficiency in more detail.

Purposeful marking means you are in control of why you are marking. It means you have a clear purpose directing your efforts; a purpose you have decided in advance and which accords with your wider motives. It may seem incongruous to talk about purposeful marking because to describe such a practice is also to suggest its opposite – marking without purpose. At first glance this seems a strange process to imply because surely all marking is driven by something, even if it is just the will to see where students are at and then return their books to them, fully marked?

I would distinguish purposeful marking as marking in which some prior thought has been exercised by the teacher regarding why they are marking, what they are marking for and how they intend their marking to have an impact.

This differs from marking which is perfunctory, or marking which is just part of the daily grind. It need not differ by much, and often it won't. The key difference, though, is that the teacher is controlling and defining their actions in pursuit of a specific goal. Let's look at some examples.

- Teacher A takes in a set of student books. They have a lot to mark but what they are really interested in is an extended piece of work completed a few days ago. The task was designed so pupils would produce material covering most of the learning from the previous few lessons. This is what the teacher focuses on, spending ninety percent of their time analysing and giving feedback on this piece of work.

- Teacher B wants to know whether their class is ready to move on or whether they need to spend a little longer looking at translation of shapes. They set a piece of work on the topic which gets progressively more challenging, take in the results and mark these. As they do, their focus is on identifying what percentage of the class have moved through the material quickly and accurately.

- Teacher C has noticed a number of misconceptions coming up in lessons. They set a piece of work designed to test which students are labouring under these. They take the books in and mark them, with the express intention of spotting who is working under the misconceptions and where this is most evident.

In each of these examples, the teacher's marking is driven by a specific purpose. This helps them to focus their efforts, elicit the information they want and take precise action in response. For example, Teacher C knows which students they need to intervene with. And they know that this intervention should focus on teaching away from misconceptions.

Purposeful marking is no great trick, then. It is simply about being mindful. When you mark – and perhaps also when you plan the work you will eventually mark – choose an overriding purpose to animate your efforts. This will increase the effectiveness of your marking by focussing your attention on useful areas. It will also increase your efficiency because the purpose you select will drive and shape your behaviour, helping to channel your effort.

Here are five further examples of purposeful marking:

- Marking in which the teacher's main aim is to see whether or not students have successfully implemented their targets.

- Marking in which the teacher intends to give feedback which tells students what to do in the next lesson.

- Marking designed to identify how effectively the teacher has taught the present topic.

- Marking in which the teacher is looking for gaps in understanding, so they can intervene and close those gaps before they grow any larger.

- Marking intended to elicit information about which students need a higher level of challenge and which are OK at the current level.

Structuring Student Work

What do you want to mark? This is a question worth considering. And we might turn it around and also ask: What do you want to give feedback on? These questions are two sides of the same coin. They both cut to the heart of what makes marking effective and efficient.

If you know what you want to mark, if you know what you want to give feedback on, then you can structure student work to achieve your goals. We briefly touched on this point in the previous section. Having a clear sense of what you are trying to achieve with your marking means there is a purpose underpinning your efforts.

You can extend this purpose out and use it to structure student work. That is, you can plan in advance what work you will ask students to produce. Through doing this, you can elicit the information you want and put yourself in a position to give feedback on the things which matter.

To illustrate this point, let us consider the position of a trainee teacher. Someone right at the beginning of their career. For this teacher, planning lessons looms large in their mind. It is a difficult task to get right, one that occupies a great deal of their thought and attention. When they take student books in they are interested to see what work has been produced, and they mark it on this basis. Indeed, part of their focus is actually on seeing whether the lessons they've planned have been well-received – whether they've had the intended impact. As such, students' work is viewed through the lens of getting to grips with lesson planning as much as anything else.

We can imagine that the trainee teacher will be pleased to see work in students' books which suggests their lessons are going down reasonably well; that they are having something like the desired effect.

But compare this situation to a more experienced teacher. Someone further into their career. We would expect this teacher to be skilled at lesson planning and to be no longer concerned about whether or not they were getting things right. Instead, this teacher's focus will have shifted from their own performance to students' performance. And they will have this in mind while planning their lessons.

This second teacher will structure their lessons so students produce the kind of work which gives a good insight into present performance. They will be able to think forward and predict what kind of tasks will give rise to what kind of work. They will be planning with marking in mind.

We can pull out two key differences between the approaches of these imaginary teachers. First, our more experienced teacher conducts more effective marking. Because they have planned with marking in mind they find themselves with student work which centres on what they're interested in. Whereas the trainee teacher ends up with work that may or may not give them the insights they need to accurately assess performance and give useful feedback. Second, the experienced teacher is a more efficient marker. They know what they want, they structure student work to gain access to this and, therefore, it is easier for them to mark quickly and precisely.

To sum up, planning lessons with marking in mind is a beneficial approach. It means thinking ahead to the kind of work the structure of your lessons and assessments will give rise to. And being prepared to tweak your planning so as to gain access to what you want. There is a close connection here with purposeful marking. We might even name this section 'purposeful planning for purposeful marking.' Or, to put it in less parsimonious terms: thinking in advance about what information you want to elicit and structuring tasks and activities with the intention of drawing this information out into the open.

Tracking Progress

Tracking progress means gaining a sound understanding of where students are at and using this to construct a measurement of change over time. This is why we have mark books in which to record our summative assessments of student work.

The greatest benefit of this is that the quantification of student performance lets us make swift comparative judgements. We can see change over time in a denuded yet efficient form. It doesn't have the depth and richness of our qualitative understanding of how students' knowledge and understanding has changed, but it does offer a succinct, comparable set of reference points. This transformation of student performance into discrete pieces of data makes it easier for us to see patterns and identify trends.

Tracking progress is thus an essential feature of effective and efficient marking. If we want to maximise our positive impact on student learning, then we need to be in a position from which to accurately judge progression. The collection of data allows us to do this. It acts as a counterpart to the qualitative judgements we make. And it serves a different, but related purpose. Formative feedback gives students access to our expertise. Summative judgements recorded in mark books let us swiftly identify progress and spot relationships and changes on which we might need to act.

You can take tracking progress further than the traditional approach of just recording marks in your mark book. Here are five examples of techniques you can use to develop your marking:

- **Track feedback alongside summative data**. This requires patience and additional time on your part. When you give students feedback, make a brief note in your mark book of what this is, either alongside any summative data you have recorded or in a separate column. This is easier to achieve with a spreadsheet mark book in Excel. To simplify the process, you can develop a code for your feedback or just record the single most important point. The benefit is that, over time, you can spot patterns and relationships between your feedback and student performance. For example, whether some students are more adept at acting on your feedback than others.

- **Question-level analysis**. This is where you record the marks for individual questions as well as the overall mark. For example, a student may complete a mock exam and achieve an overall mark of 80 out of 100. Question-level analysis means you record both this mark and the marks achieved by the student on each question. You can then identify underperformance in specific areas. One Year 6 teacher, for example, might use question-level analysis with their learners during mock SATS and discover that most of the class are underperforming on a particular question type. Armed with this information, they are in a position to remedy the situation.

- **Redefine what progress means**. You may decide that progress needs a broader definition than just improvement in test scores. If so, you then have a different conceptual basis for recording information about student performance. For example, an art teacher might choose to redefine progress so it takes account of the subjective elements of artistic judgement. Having done this, they would then find themselves tracking different information about student performance – information arising from their changed understanding of progress – than was previously the case, with different implications for feedback, interventions and lesson planning.

- **Link target implementation to summative data**. We have already stressed the importance of giving students an opportunity to implement their targets. You can embed the importance of this in your progress tracking by linking target implementation to summative data. For example, you might have two rows of inputs for each student. The first is for summative data based on their most recent piece of work. The second is a tick, cross or circle indicating whether they have met their target, not met their target or made some progress towards their target.

- **Rapid interventions**. This is where we intervene as soon as we feel students are falling behind their peers. Instead of waiting to analyse student learning over a longer period of time, we step in earlier in an effort to prevent problems growing. In terms of progress tracking, this can mean making more summative judgements – perhaps with each of these being based on smaller pieces of work – so as to spot patterns sooner. Or, it can mean using summative data in your mark book as an additional piece of information which either supports or goes against the qualitative judgements you make in lessons, based on your observations of student learning.

Communicating with Students

Marking communicates information to students. Effective marking communicates the information the teacher wants to communicate and does so in a form which students can access. Different types of information can be communicated – a tick or a cross, a detailed comment or even a simple question mark. In all cases, efficacy will drop if the student doesn't understand what the information means or if the teacher has attempted to communicate one thing but the student has interpreted something different.

The most obvious consequence of this is that we should pay attention to the cogency of that element of our marking which communicates information to students. Often this is straightforward and requires little extra effort on our part. In certain cases, however, the situation alters. This is especially true of formative feedback, where there is an emphasis on students decoding and internalising the information presented to them in written form.

There is an impact on efficiency as well. If learners do not understand the information we are seeking to convey, or if they misunderstand that information, then we will have to do additional work further down the line. Either in the form of supplementary explanation (though this is not always a bad thing) or in trying to work out how students incorrectly interpreted our feedback and what unforeseen consequences this has had.

We've already looked at the importance of clarity when delivering feedback, so let's put that to one side. An area we can focus on instead is training students in how to respond to your marking.

Training differs from teaching in that it is more about habituating learners into a way of acting which they can repeat in the future. Here we are thinking about how we can train learners to analyse and interpret the information our marking contains.

For example, a teacher taking on a new class may spend some time talking to students about why they mark, how they mark and what sort of information their marking communicates. They might then go on to outline how they would like students to engage with this information. How they would like them to think about it and use it.

This teacher might provide students with a small handout summarising what they've said. It might contain information such as the following:

- If you see a question mark, this means I don't understand what you've written. You need to look at this again and either change it or explain to me what it means.

- A cross means the answer is wrong. Your challenge is to try to identify why it's wrong. Then we'll talk about it together.

- In my comments, I'll always write strengths first, then a target. You can use a highlighter to pick out the target so it's easier to spot in your book.

Each of these statements is an articulation of a rule the teacher wants students to follow. The aim is to minimise ambiguity, maximise efficiency and, as a result, ensure their marking is as effective as possible.

Taking an approach such as this at the start of the year – or whenever you pick up a new class – can save a lot of time and effort further down the line. It also means learners know what to expect. They can start to predict what they will see when they get their work back. This speeds things up and helps develop a sense that marking and feedback is always a two-way process – a collaborative endeavour aimed at helping students to get better.

Finally, remember that the aim of training is to make a habit second nature. If you adopt this approach, you will need to put more into it early on; as time passes, students will internalise the information and won't need you to remind them of it. They will become habituated to how you communicate through your marking.

Criteria and Judgement

When you mark you judge. Marking is judgement. As a teacher becomes more experienced, so they tend to mark more efficiently. This is largely because they have a better understanding of what good looks like, of what they want to see from their students and of what problems, errors, misconceptions and mistakes look like. Over time, the teacher builds up an increasingly detailed, increasingly nuanced understanding which they use to make quicker, better and more accurate judgements.

Judgements centre on an act of comparison. We look at student work and compare it to what we know. This knowledge encompasses many things, including:

- Knowledge of the curriculum

- Knowledge of past work we have seen from students

- Knowledge of what we expect students to be doing at this point of time – both as individuals (based on learners' past performance) and in general (based on a wider understanding of learning and progress)

- Knowledge of what good looks like

- Knowledge of what is likely and what is unlikely (which helps us spot plagiarism, for example)

We can increase the effectiveness and efficiency of our marking by attending to the criteria we use to make judgements. This means we accept the idea that judgement involves an act of comparison and then focus our attention on the knowledge we use to make that comparison. Here are five techniques you can apply:

- If you are an early-career teacher, reflect on your marking once you have done it. Ask yourself how you made your judgements. What did you do to assess student work? What comparisons were you making? Did you use external criteria such as a mark-scheme, or internal criteria that you carry in your own mind? Did you identify a particularly good piece of work and a weaker one and use these as reference points? Could you have done anything differently? If so, what? Reflecting in this way helps you attend directly to the information and processes you use to make your judgements. You can then use them more efficaciously in the future – or even change how you are doing things.

- Create a piece of exemplar work – one for which you would give full marks – and keep this on hand while you mark. You can use it as a reference point for making judgements. It becomes an ideal against which to assess students' work. One caveat is that you should ensure your exemplar work is relevant for the age group you are working with. If the exemplar is too good then you risk setting up a situation in which none of your students can gain full marks, because none will be able to fully match your exemplar.

- Make a list of the key criteria you use to make judgements when you mark. Spend a bit of time thinking about the main categories you attend to when looking at student work. For example, a philosophy teacher might always call on the categories of clarity, consistency and logic. Articulating the criteria you use to make judgements means better understanding how the process of marking works for you. It also means having a list on which to call while you mark. This frees up space in your working memory. You do not have to keep switching your attention from analysing student work to thinking about how you will judge it.

- Begin with mistakes in mind. For example, a maths teacher will have an excellent knowledge of the common mistakes learners make when starting out with long division. By bringing these mistakes to the forefront of their mind they are primed to spot them. They have picked out a key aspect against which they make judgements and can focus on applying this across the range of work they mark. This approach is particularly useful if you have a given aspect – such as mistake-making – on which you want to focus and about which you believe feedback will be particularly useful for your students.

- Take a minute or two before you mark to clarify your expectations. For example, you might identify that you have especially high expectations of the set of books you are about to mark and then make a mental note of why this is the case. Or, you might refine your expectations of what good looks like for work of this type. Either way, you are taking a moment to sharpen your focus, so that when you come to make judgements you know exactly what you are looking for and, by extension, what work which does not match up to your expectations looks like as well.

When to Mark and When Not to Mark

We conclude the chapter by turning to the idea of discrimination. When to mark – and when not to mark.

Time is at a premium for any teacher. You must spend your time well if you want to get the most from it. This means you must prioritise. You must decide what you will mark and into what marking you will put the most effort. You cannot mark everything and you certainly cannot mark everything to the same degree. Discrimination – judgement – must be exercised. Without this, your workload will be immense. Unsustainable. And this will have a negative impact on you as a person, on your enjoyment of the job and, quite possibly, on your students.

After all, the one place where you can have the biggest impact on your learners, and therefore where you need the most energy available to use, is in the classroom, while you are teaching. So if you find yourself marking endlessly, devoting hours and hours to it, stop. Consider the consequences of what you are doing. And also consider the cost-benefit of how you are approaching the task.

There is no doubt that marking suffers from diminishing returns. After a point, the more you do, the less you and your students get out of it. This goes back in part to some of the previous points we discussed around communication, manageability and relevance. If students are faced with an excess of feedback, they will struggle to take it all in, may disengage, or may simply pass over the most salient points. (This response is not too different from the kind of response we would have if faced with a similar situation.)

I cannot tell you what you should mark and what you shouldn't mark. It is influenced by who you are teaching, what age group you're working with, the topics you teach, where you are in the academic year and more besides. But, I can stress the importance of you making judgements about when to mark and when not to mark. About applying your professional discernment to work out what will bring the biggest benefit to students for the effort you'll need to put in. Sometimes this means low effort from you and high benefits for students. Sometimes your effort, and the extent of the marking, will need to be greater. But there is certainly no definite link between *excessive* marking and better progress.

So what can you do to make good decisions? To exercise your judgement in a manner which leads to positive results? Three things are worth thinking about:

1) What information do I want to communicate to students through my marking, and how will they use that information?

2) What information do I want to elicit through my marking, and how will I use that?

3) How will my marking positively influence student learning, and what evidence supports my view?

These three questions are an excellent starting point for deciding what to prioritise. They tally with much of what has been said in the book so far. They may not give you all the answers, but they will take you a long way towards working out what the best use of your time is – for your own benefit and the benefit of students.

Another thing to consider is structuring student work, something we spoke about earlier in the chapter. If you plan what to mark, as was suggested there, then it is more likely that your marking will be efficient and your time well spent. You will be exercising your judgement in advance of the event, with the intention of facilitating work which is worth marking and which allows you to convey rich, timely and useful information to your students, as well as to track their progress.

With those thoughts in mind, we draw this chapter to a close. We will return to marking in Chapter Five, when we look in detail at written feedback. First, though, we'll turn to the spoken variety.

Chapter Four – Verbal Feedback

Introduction

If the first three chapters have laid the groundwork, while maintaining a sharply practical edge, the remainder of the book builds on them and further increases the practical emphasis. In this chapter we examine a range of strategies, activities and techniques you can use to deliver effective verbal feedback. That is, feedback which tallies with most or all of the points raised in Chapters 1 and 2.

Pre- and Post-Activity Feedback

Activities are the main feature of lessons. This is where much of the learning happens. We can give verbal feedback before and after activities, to individuals, groups or the class as a whole. Both methods have their benefits; both give us an opportunity to share expert information with learners, information that can drive their efforts and influence their approach. Here are some examples:

- **Pre-Activity Feedback 1.** If you regularly use a specific activity and know the kind of problems students can get into, or the kind of errors which tend to be committed, use this information as the basis for pre-activity feedback. This sees you using feedback to signal to learners where they should target their efforts and what to look out for during the activity itself. It also means you can refer back to the feedback during the activity if students forget about it or go off task.

- **Pre-Activity Feedback 2.** Identify a single learner or a group of learners you feel will benefit from some extra support in the upcoming activity. Provide this to them in the form of pre-activity feedback. Think ahead and predict where these learners might get into difficulties, then deliver feedback before the event. This method gives learners a leg-up, helping them to understand how best to tackle a task before they get bogged down in the practicalities of doing it. A simple example is a PE teacher explaining to a group of less-able rugby players the importance of maintaining defensive shape even when they are tired, and giving them a mental cue to use as a reminder.

- **Post-Activity Feedback 1.** During the course of an activity, circulate through the room and identify any common themes running throughout the class. These could be positive things which attract praise and also areas which suggest a need for improvement. At the end of the activity, instead of moving on straightaway, spend some time talking to your learners about what you observed. Use this as an opportunity to give feedback to the group as a whole. You might team this up with an opportunity for reflection, give learners a chance to redo part of the activity, or model the improvements you feel could be made.

- **Post-Activity Feedback 2.** Identify a group of learners who found the activity easy, or who appeared to be coasting. Give feedback to these learners which increases the level of challenge moving forwards. This could mean the feedback challenges them to think more deeply or work harder in the next section of the lesson. Or, it could be feedback which prompts them to work differently the next time you use an activity of this type. Either way, you are using the information elicited during the course of the activity to deliver feedback which influences students' future efforts.

A more general point to make about pre-activity feedback is that it helps shape students' interactions with the activity. For this reason, it is a good tool to call on if you feel there is potential for the activity to fall short of what you had in mind when you planned it. In terms of post-activity feedback, the impact can be intensified by planning a lesson section which goes: Activity -> Feedback -> Activity. Here, we run the activity, give post-activity feedback, then run a second activity in which individuals, groups or the class as a whole act on this.

Mid-Activity Feedback

Mid-activity feedback is perhaps the most common form of verbal feedback. The one we use the most when teaching. This is where we give learners feedback while they are engaged in activities, with the intention of helping them to perform better, think deeper and do things differently than would otherwise be the case. Here are some strategies and techniques you can use to finesse your practice:

1. Identify in advance a handful of students to whom you would like to give feedback. During the activity, call these students up to your desk, one at a time. Spend a few minutes talking to them about their work and delivering the feedback you feel will best help them.

2. If students are working in groups, ask each group to appoint an envoy. Explain that during the course of the activity you will call up envoys from different groups. They should come to the front of the room to discuss their group's work with you, whereupon you will provide feedback for them to take back and deliver to their peers.

3. Choose one thing you want to give feedback on. For example, misconceptions, sentence structure or use of line when drawing. Circulate through the room and give feedback to as many students as you like, but always keeping to the topic you identified at the beginning. Not only does this benefit the students through the provision of expert information, but it also lets you focus your mind on a single area of your expertise.

4. Sometimes it is useful to stop the activity mid-flow and deliver feedback to the whole class. Learners can take a moment to reflect on this before you set the activity running again. You should then circulate and observe whether or not learners are acting on the feedback you gave. This is particularly useful if an activity is proving more difficult than you anticipated or if many learners are making similar mistakes.

5. Circulate through the room holding a piece of paper and a pen. When you spot a student who will benefit from your feedback, use these to help you communicate effectively. This sees you supplementing your verbal feedback with written or visual information. For example, a geography teacher might give a learner feedback on how to talk more analytically about migration flows, then draw them a quick diagram as a reminder.

6. Create a class set of lollipop sticks. Each stick should have a different student's name on it. During activities, draw out sticks at random and give feedback to the students you select. This approach is a modification of an

AfL technique. It means you avoid unconscious biases. For example, you might unwittingly find yourself giving feedback to students who sit in the middle of the room more than those on the edges. The lollipop method can help avoid this problem arising.

7. Keep a list in your head of those students who would most benefit from an increased level of challenge. When the activity is up and running, visit each of these students in turn and give them a piece of feedback which will stretch their thinking or abilities. For example, an English teacher might set up a persuasive writing activity, let it run for a short while, and then visit five students in turn, using feedback to increase the level of challenge for each one.

Feedback as Scaffolding

You can use verbal feedback to scaffold student learning in a variety of ways. Here are five examples:

- **A learner is struggling to get started with a task.** Feedback can take the form of advice on how to begin the task, it can summarise how students have successfully started tasks in the past, or it can suggest a specific target the student can pursue which, when achieved, will mean they've successfully started the task. For example, a history teacher might summarise the good things they've seen a student do in previous source analysis tasks before asking them to apply the same process to the present task.

- **A learner is finding it difficult to improve their work.** Here the teacher can scaffold the learning by doing something on behalf of the learner – effectively analysing what they have done so far. If a learner is finding it hard to improve their work, then it suggests they are also finding it hard to successfully assess what they have done. After all, if they could effectively critique what's in front of them then they would be in a position to make improvements. The teacher does this on their behalf and delivers feedback focussing on what could be done to deliver some improvements. The student is then in a position to act on this information.

- **A learner is repeatedly making the same mistakes but can't work out why.** This may be because they aren't aware of the mistakes they're making or because they don't quite have the knowledge and understanding necessary to pick apart what is happening. The teacher steps in, delivering verbal feedback which doesn't solve the student's problem but gives them enough feedback so that they can fix it themselves. For example, a maths student might be factorising quadratic equations and consistently making the same mistake. The teacher steps in and provides verbal feedback based on their own expertise which nudges the student in the right direction. They then take this and generate a solution for themselves.

- **A learner is unable to use their target.** Perhaps because they don't understand it or perhaps because they cannot see how it can be applied to the task in hand. The teacher observes what is happening and steps in to help. They provide the learner with feedback which has a dual purpose. First, it re-explains what their target is and why it matters. Second, it highlights some of the links between their target and the task they are trying to complete. The learner is then a position to take things on themselves and experience a greater sense of success in applying their target.

- **A learner is trying to achieve something but keeps falling it short.** The likelihood is that they will not understand why they are falling short or how to bridge the gap. Here, the teacher offers verbal feedback which directs the student to try something different; something the teacher knows will go a long way towards helping them achieve what they are trying to achieve. For example, in a textiles lesson, the teacher sees a student struggling to create a shape they want, so they provide some expert verbal feedback which unpicks why they are falling short and what changes they might like to try – the implicit message being that these changes will give rise to a different outcome.

Teaching Away from Mistakes

Mistakes are one of the main ways in which we learn. They often present information which helps us to make significant alterations to our thinking and the ways in which we act. Focussing verbal feedback on mistakes means drawing students' attention to these before providing the information needed to understand why they have made them, what they can learn from them and how to avoid repeating them in the future. Here are four techniques you can use:

- **Identify mistakes in advance.** You are an expert in the areas you teach. Therefore you will probably be able to identify in advance the kind of mistakes students are likely to make. If you do this – either by making a brief list or by running through the possibilities in your mind – you are then primed to spot the mistakes as and when students make them. This leaves you ready to intervene and offer feedback. For example, a Year 5 teacher introducing a new topic might think back to the time they taught it last year, make a mental note of the common mistakes they remember students making, and then be in a position to swiftly give relevant verbal feedback should they see the same mistakes cropping up again.

- **Probe for misconceptions.** Use questioning to probe student understanding during activities. Focus on trying to draw out any misconceptions students hold about the learning. Once these are out in the open, you are in a position to offer feedback which can help students change how they think. For example, a religious studies teacher might probe students' understanding of a religion with which they have little familiarity. Through doing this they draw out misconceptions the student holds about that religion and can give feedback in response.

- **Observe and intervene.** During activities, stand in a position from which you can observe the whole class. Or, depending on what you are teaching, you might prefer to circulate so you can more closely scrutinise the work students are doing. On spotting a mistake, take this as an opportunity to intervene – to provide verbal feedback which can help improve student performance. Do give consideration to the frequency of your interventions, though. For example, a student who receives feedback from you three or four times in a matter of minutes may start to see your feedback in a negative light.

- **Verbal feedback after written feedback.** Having handed out student work which you have marked and which contains your feedback, circulate through the room and identify any students who would benefit from further verbal feedback focussing on the mistakes they made. For example, a maths teacher might pick out two or three learners who need clarification of the written feedback to feel confident about acting on it. The teacher does this by verbally re-explaining the feedback and how it relates to the mistakes students have made.

Feedback on Student Thinking

When giving verbal feedback during lessons, one useful area on which you can focus is student thinking. This means providing information students can use to think differently, to change their thinking or to think in ways they were otherwise ignoring. The common factor in all cases is that we are giving access to our expertise as a thinker, and using this to shepherd and mould the thinking students do. Here are some exemplar techniques:

'I'd like you to think about X' Here the teacher gives feedback which asks students to think about something they have overlooked or ignored. It can be delivered as a brief instruction or with additional information explaining why 'X' is worth thinking about and what the student can expect to discover by pursuing this path. For example, a science teacher might say to a student: 'I'd like you to think about the way the different surfaces affect the amount of friction. There might be a pattern there, waiting to be discovered.' This encourages the student to think about something they were otherwise ignoring – and the teacher knows that positive results are likely to ensue.

'I'd like you to try thinking about it this way…' In this formulation, the teacher gives the student access to their expert thinking. They know there is a better, or perhaps just a different, way of thinking about the subject, and so they encourage the student to take that path. For example, a philosophy teacher might say to a student: 'I'd like you to try thinking about justice in this way: Imagine that you didn't have the capacity to think about consequences. How might your conception of the idea be different from what you think now?'

'Try thinking about how X connects to Y.' For example: 'Try thinking about how probability connects to insurance.' Or: 'Try thinking about how Goldilocks connects to our local area.' In both cases, the feedback is designed to get the student making connections they might otherwise have missed. This promotion of lateral thinking is easy for the teacher because of their expert knowledge. But it is harder for students to achieve because of their more novice position. Verbal feedback of this type can open up ideas for students and give access to ways of thinking that might otherwise have remained inaccessible.

'Try thinking about this first, then that.' If a student is struggling to get to grips with a task or idea, it may be because their working memory is overloaded. Too much new information can slow down a student's ability to process what's in front of them. Even to the point that they stop what they are doing and disengage completely. You can make life easier for them by giving verbal feedback on their thinking using this formulation. For example: 'Try thinking about the key features of the landscape first, before deciding how you want to use colour.' Or: 'Try thinking about what you want to say first, then decide how you will say it.'

'I'd like you to write down your thoughts and then refine them.' This is a good way to help students exert a higher degree of control over their thinking. Writing thoughts down means externalising them and fixing them in time and space. Having done this – having articulated what they are thinking – the student is in a position to look critically at these and decide how they can refine them. For example, a Year 6 teacher might ask a student to write down their thoughts about a book they are reading, and then to refine these. This is in contrast to the student holding the thoughts in their mind or attempting to put them directly into a piece of writing, without the additional step of articulation and refinement.

Re-directing Student Effort

One of the more subtle uses of verbal feedback is the re-direction of student effort. I say 'subtle' because students often aren't fully aware of what you are doing when you use it in this way. Or, if they are aware, they understand implicitly that this is the game and that they should follow what you are suggesting. This stands in contrast to the odd occasion in which a student will push against any attempt to re-direct their efforts. While rare, this can happen. But it is usually a result of an underlying issue connected to behaviour, as opposed to anything inherently wrong with the technique.

Here are some examples of verbal feedback which re-directs student effort:

- 'Back on task now, Sam. Thanks very much.'

- 'Let's get thinking about the third question again. I'll be back in two minutes to see what ideas you have.'

- 'I wonder if there's a better way to do this? Come on – I want you to have a look and find out for me.'

- 'Interesting approach, Sarah, but I'd like to see you following the method to begin with.'

- 'Now this could be a more useful avenue to pursue. Try it out and I'll be interested to hear what you think.'

- 'Let's park that question and discuss it after the lesson. Right now, I want you to focus on the task.'

- 'Remind me of the instructions. Right, so let's keep those in mind for the rest of the activity.'

- 'Is this the right way to do it? No? OK, so what is the right way? Perfect! Off you go then.'

- 'I think this might be a dead end. Why don't you try going back and having another look. See if the third bullet point gives you any ideas.'

- 'Remember what we talked about last lesson? That's right – keeping focussed.'

In each example the teacher's aim is to change the direction of student effort. Some of them are procedural, some behavioural and some concerned with thinking about how to tackle a task. This reflects the wide variety of reasons why students might lose focus, or might direct their efforts in unproductive ways.

There is overlap here with some of our other points about verbal feedback. For example, feedback on student thinking, which comes very close to a couple of the exemplar sentences above. What should be noted, however, is that verbal feedback intended to re-direct student effort is often briefer in nature and more specifically concerned with what students are doing in the moment. Good practice tends to involve the teacher regularly scanning the room during tasks, looking to see whose effort levels are low, whose effort is being expended in unhelpful directions, and who might benefit from a brief reminder or passing suggestion about what they should be doing.

In conclusion, verbal feedback of this type is as much about you helping students to self-regulate their own effort as anything else.

Feedback on Progress

Giving verbal feedback on progress is a good way to help students gain a better understanding of how they are getting on with a task. This can be particularly useful for students who struggle to perceive their own progress and those who do not believe that they are capable of making much or any progress.

For example, we might have a learner who doubts their ability in literacy. They do not believe they have what it takes to get better and feel there is little chance of them making progress. These features are characteristic of a fixed mindset, in which the learner's experience of learning is influenced by the guiding beliefs they have about themselves and what constitutes intelligence, ability and talent more widely.

As a teacher, we want this student to develop a more realistic view of themselves – one in which they acknowledge the possibility for change, growth and development. We want them to start seeing themselves as we see them. That is, as someone who can make progress and get better by putting in effort, seeking support and learning from mistakes. We know from working with them that they can do well and have done well. What we now need to do is communicate this message to them.

So we decide to give them verbal feedback about the progress they are making in individual lessons and across a sequence of lessons, using some or all of the following strategies:

1. During lessons, we speak to the student on a number of occasions, each time drawing their attention to the progress they are making and explaining that this is a result of the decisions they've made and the effort they've put in.

2. When the student doesn't make the kind of progress we would like, we use verbal feedback to focus their attention on what they could do differently to change things. We work collaboratively with them and stop them from fixating on the idea that lack of progress is due to an inherent lack of ability.

3. We use a scale to help the student talk to us about how much progress they feel they are making. A simple scale running from 1-10, where 1 means no progress and 10 means excellent progress, will suffice. We can then give the student verbal feedback explaining what progress *we* believe they are making, linking this to the scale.

4. After a few lessons have passed, we work one-on-one with the student, looking back over their work and giving them verbal feedback explaining how they have made progress, why they have made progress and what evidence there is to support this view.

5. At the end of a unit of work we take a few moments to speak to the student, comparing where they were at when the unit began to where they are now. We point to the evidence in their work demonstrating the progress they've made. Our feedback helps the student gain a more accurate, more realistic picture of what they have done and where they've been successful.

In each of these strategies, the underlying aim is to draw students' perception of themselves and their work closer to our perception. We are giving them access to our expertise as a teacher – our ability to objectively analyse what students do, how they think and the possibilities which are open to them. Over time, verbal feedback of this type can have a powerful influence on students, changing how they see themselves and what they think is possible when it comes to learning and achievement.

Real-Time Verbal Feedback

In some settings, real-time verbal feedback can be a huge benefit by providing students with information they can use to modify their thinking and behaviour in the moment. By real-time we mean feedback which is almost a narration of what students are doing, followed by an immediate opportunity to act on this, and then by further feedback in response. This differs from other examples of verbal feedback we've looked at in the chapter, where it is assumed that the student has already done something (as opposed to 'is doing something') to which we respond.

Here are some examples:

- **PE**: The teacher cycles round the edge of the track while a group of able students are running a 1500 metre time-trial. The teacher observes how the students are running and gives them real-time feedback on body position, posture and cadence. Students react to this in the moment, making adjustments to what they are doing. The teacher continues to cycle alongside, making further observations and offering more feedback. Again, students have a chance to apply this in real-time.

- **Design and Technology**: The teacher works with a student who is using a tool for the first time. They begin by giving a demonstration and then provide the student with real-time feedback as they try to use the tool correctly. The teacher narrates the student's efforts, drawing their attention to subtle changes they need to make to improve what they are doing. This means the student gains real-time access to the teacher's expertise and can use this to modify their use of the tool.

- **Dance**: A dance teacher works with a group of students who are practising a routine they have choreographed. The dance teacher steps in and joins the group. They slow the routine down and lead the students through it, narrating what they are doing as they go. The teacher gives special emphasis to any discrepancies between their own performance and what the students are doing. They are then in a position to act on this feedback in real-time, as they work with the teacher.

- **Maths**: A Year 4 teacher sits down with one of their learners and asks them to talk through how they are trying to solve some of the sums they've been set. The teacher listens to the learner's explanation and starts to narrate back to them what they have said. The learner then takes on the role of listener and the teacher talks them through an alternative approach. The learner has a go at this approach while the teacher narrates what is happening. As they do this, they help the learner to get their application right by talking them through any trial and error which crops up.

- **French**: A French teacher engages a student in a one-on-one conversation. As the conversation progresses, the teacher gives feedback on what the student is saying and how they are saying it, while also maintaining the conversation in French. The two processes continue simultaneously, meaning the student is both practising their French and gaining real-time feedback they can use to improve the quality of their speaking.

Each example demonstrates a different application of real-time verbal feedback. All achieve similar results. Students gain access to information they can use to modify and adapt what they are doing in the moment, thus improving their performance. An additional benefit is that the teacher can respond to the modifications students make, potentially speeding up the process of improvement.

Using a Structure to Underpin Verbal Feedback

Sometimes you might find yourself unsure how to pitch your verbal feedback. The pace of the lesson and the number of things requiring your attention can compound the issue. A good fall-back in such situations is to use a structure to underpin your verbal feedback. The structure does the work in advance; you only need to find the appropriate element of it and then use this to formulate feedback that is relevant and useful to the student in front of you. Here are five examples you can call on:

- **Bloom's Taxonomy of the Cognitive Domain.** This is the taxonomy with which most teachers are familiar. It delineates cognitive processes into a hierarchy of six categories: knowledge, comprehension, application, analysis, synthesis, evaluation. Each category is progressively more challenging than the last. You can call on the taxonomy when delivering verbal feedback. Simply ask yourself where the student appears to be at and which category would therefore present them with a challenge, were you to base your feedback on it.

- **Taxonomies of the Psycho-Motor Domain.** When the taxonomy of the cognitive domain was put together in the 1950s, thought was also given to taxonomies of the affective domain and the psycho-motor domain. A handbook of the former was published in the 1960s, but no handbook appeared for the latter. Subsequent writers have developed different taxonomies of the psycho-motor domain, however. One of these, by Dave (1971), ranks the categories of psychomotor development as: imitation, manipulation, precision, articulation, naturalisation. This structure is useful to call on when teaching practical subjects, as it tends to provide a better basis for constructing feedback than the taxonomy of the cognitive domain. You might also like to consider the category of invention as being beyond naturalisation – wherein the learner starts to invent new uses of the skill they have naturalised.

- **Concrete to Abstract.** By and large, concrete ideas and information are simpler to comprehend than abstract ones. We can imagine a continuum running from 'completely concrete' at one end to 'completely abstract' at the other. With this in mind, we can seek to place our feedback at a point along the continuum which feels most appropriate for the learner in front of us. For example, we might find a learner who is struggling to get to grips with the basics of a task. In this situation, our verbal feedback will be better placed towards the 'completely concrete' end of the continuum than anywhere else.

- **General to Specific.** Another continuum to have in your mind is general to specific. This one runs from 'highly general' at one end to 'highly specific' at the other. Arguably, as you get more specific the level of challenge increases. Though this is not always the case and you should consider carefully the application of this structure, bearing in mind what students are studying. When appropriate, it is another useful tool you can call on to structure your verbal feedback. For example, you might find a learner who is breezing through a task and decide that highly specific feedback will cause them to slow down and look more carefully at what they are doing. You thus use your feedback to raise the level of challenge and push the learner to think differently.

- **Mark-Schemes.** The final structuring tool to suggest is the mark-scheme relevant to the work students are doing. If you have a copy of this to hand – or are sufficiently familiar with it to have it stored in your mind – then you can use it to frame the verbal feedback you provide. This might see you giving feedback based on certain parts of the mark-scheme, or providing feedback which encourages students to think and work in ways which are more in line with the demands of the mark-scheme. Either way, you are using the mark-scheme as an underpinning framework.

Other structuring tools are available – and I'm sure you're familiar with ones not mentioned here. They can all be used for the same end. Namely, increasing the likelihood that the verbal feedback you give is tailored to the student in front of you. The structuring tool does some of the work for you; especially useful when you are under pressure or your attention is divided.

That ends our chapter on verbal feedback. We will look at some additional ideas elsewhere, especially in Chapter Seven – Further Feedback Techniques. For now, let us move on to examine some practical strategies for high-quality written feedback.

Chapter Five – Written Feedback

Introduction: Strengths and Targets

Written feedback predominantly comprises information which can be divided into one of two categories: strengths and targets. Strengths are the things the learner has done well. The target is the thing the learner needs to do next, either to improve their work in the future or in direct response to the work the teacher has marked.

The permanence of writing means written feedback remains accessible over time. This contrasts with the ephemeral nature of verbal feedback which, once spoken, disappears. As a result, many teachers use written feedback as a more formal measure than the verbal counterpart, providing it to students on a regular basis, in response to having marked their work, and using it as a formative summary of where the student is at and where they need to go next.

It is widely held that students benefit from a number of pieces of positive information before being given something to work on. Hence why many teachers provide three strengths and a target. This means the positive information outweighs the constructively critical information. Another advantage of providing strengths, though, is that it signals to learners what good looks like – and therefore what they should continue doing that they are doing already.

Positive reinforcement of this type helps learners develop a better understanding of what the success criteria are that you use to judge their work. Over time, it is hoped, they will build up an increasingly accurate understanding of what you expect from them, based in no small part on the information relayed through your feedback. This includes the information contained in the targets you give as well as the strengths you note.

Too much written feedback can make life difficult for students. They need time and space to act on the information you provide. If they are bombarded with strengths and targets it can become hard for them to assimilate everything you are trying to communicate. In the case of targets it can also mean they struggle to successfully apply what you are asking them to do – because another target has suddenly arrived and their focus has now switched to this.

Thinking about assimilation, it is important to remember that students need time in which they can read through your feedback, reflect on it and also act on it. This is an obvious point – but I have seen many teachers hand back work containing written feedback and then immediately move the lesson onto something new. Without time in which to engage with feedback, students are likely to ignore it, forget about it or simply assume that it is not that important – with this assumption based on the implicit message sent by the teacher's decision not to give time over to engaging with it.

It is also worth remembering that your expertise places you in a position from which you can give all students comprehensive, highly detailed feedback covering almost every aspect of their work. This is a trap you must be careful to avoid. A significant part of providing written feedback is synthesising the information you gain from marking student work and combining this with your expert knowledge and understanding, before giving students the feedback which will be of most use to them. Letting your expertise take over means you run the risk of overwhelming students. Too much information, while a result of good intentions, will overload students, causing them to withdraw or spend an excessive amount of time trying to unpick what you have written.

In the rest of this chapter we will look at different techniques you can call on to enhance the quality and efficacy of your written feedback. It should be noted here that the points made in Chapters Two and Three continue to apply and that you might also like to see this chapter as a complement to the one which follows, where we take an in depth look at targets.

Opening Up Success Criteria

Success criteria are the things against which work is judged. If you hit the success criteria – or surpass them – then fantastic. If you fall short, then you have something you need to work on. Feedback helps students understand success criteria. Strengths signal what is good and therefore desired. Targets signal that which is yet to be achieved but which will be beneficial if it is achieved. In both cases, information is conveyed about what the teacher is judging student work against.

Here are two ways in which you can use written feedback to effectively open up success criteria:

- **Use 'because'**. As soon as you include this word in your feedback you can be almost guaranteed that your sentence is explaining to the learner why something is the case. Through this explanation you justify the strength or target you have given. This justification connects to the success criteria on which you have called to make your judgement. Compare these two written strengths to demonstrate the point:

A) Your use of adjectives is really impressive.

B) Your use of adjectives is really impressive because you've thought carefully about where to place them and the impact they'll have on the reader.

The second example contains far more information. The sentence pivots on the word 'because'. In so doing, it signals to the learner why the strength is a strength. The success criteria you are using to make judgements is invoked. The learner has direct access to your sense of what good looks like. They can assimilate the semantic content of the feedback as well as the strength itself. In future, they are more likely to remember why the strength is a strength.

- **Connect targets to future success.** When we give a target we do so because we know that if the learner successfully implements it then their work will improve. Our aim is to help them understand how they can change their work for the better. The target is our call to action, directing the student's future effort. To help them understand more clearly why this matters, we can connect targets to future success. This helps the learner to appreciate the success criteria we are using to make judgements. Compare these examples to demonstrate the point:

A) Next time, I'd like you to focus on drawing your own conclusions from your findings.

B) Next time, I'd like you to focus on drawing your own conclusions from your findings. This will make your write-up more successful by demonstrating that you can interpret the data using what you know about the topic.

As with the previous example, more information is conveyed in (B) than in (A). But note how the target is contextualised in light of what successful implementation will give rise to. The teacher is explaining to the student why the target matters; what it will lead to that is not happening at present. This makes life easier for the learner. The target no longer exists in isolation. Instead, it exists in relation to a reason for its being communicated. The learner now knows the what and the why. It is the why which gives access to the success criteria.

Normalising Challenge

If we find ourselves challenged then the likelihood is that we are learning or, at least, in a position from which to learn. This is because something is a challenge if we can't do it with ease. And if we can't do it with ease then we need to learn about what we are faced with in order to be able to do it with ease in the future. To put it another way, a challenge arises when we are pushed towards the edge of what we can presently do.

Normalising challenge means habituating students into seeing it as a standard part of your lessons. The second step is to get them to embrace challenge. This is more likely if they see challenge as the norm. If they do, and if they embrace it as a result, then they will make better progress – because they will be continually pushing themselves to go beyond what they can currently do.

We can use written feedback to normalise challenge. Here are three ways in which to do it:

- **Set challenging targets.** You can do this in a number of ways. First, you can set a target and then ask yourself how you can tweak it to make it more challenging. Second, you can set a target which requires students to think again about what they thought they already knew. Third, you can ask students to change something on which they rely – such as an approach to planning. Fourth, you can set a target based on knowledge or understanding which is beyond what students are presently dealing with. Fifth, you can ask students to do something with a much higher level of accuracy than is presently the case. We could go on, but that is enough to get you started. As important as setting challenging targets is setting them regularly and giving students the time, space and support necessary to successfully implement them.

- **Focus feedback on the level of challenge.** This sees you commenting in your written feedback on how students have responded to the level of challenge, whether it is too low or too high, and what might be preferable moving forwards. For example, you might indicate that the high proportion of strengths evidenced in a student's work is a sign that the level of challenge was too low. So, you would write, this means that next time it will need to be increased. This could then form the basis of the target you set. For example, you might ask the student in question to tell you if the work is too easy – during the course of the lesson – so that you can make changes on the spot and ensure that the level of challenge is sufficiently high to push their thinking.

- **Challenge students to take the lead.** Instead of doing all the work for the student through your feedback, do some of it and then pass ownership over. Provide students with a comment about what they have done well and then ask them to tell you how they could improve their work. Follow this up with the suggestion that they make changes based on what they have identified – either to the work just produced or to the next piece they create. Some learners may require a little extra support during this process. One option is to note down three areas and then ask them to pick one they feel is ripe for improvement. They then develop a target based on the area they selected – which is slightly simpler than doing all the work themselves.

Creating a Culture of Improvement

Your written feedback will play a bigger role in students' learning if you create a culture of improvement in your classroom. By this, I mean a culture in which students understand that they can improve their work, that improvement is something to be striven for, and that making changes based on the feedback they receive is a positive thing.

This can run counter to some students' existing perceptions. A common experience for many teachers is the student who finds it difficult to see feedback in a positive light – who gets defensive when told they could improve something and seeks to withdraw from the feedback rather than embrace it.

Written feedback can exacerbate such tendencies because of its fixed and seemingly immutable nature. The comments are written on the student's work, set rigid for all to see. This contrasts to verbal feedback where information is spoken and then disappears. Feedback of this type tends to feel less threatening to those students who assume (falsely) that critical feedback is some kind of rebuke.

Creating a culture of improvement is often about changing how these students think. Altering their perceptions so they start to see the written information you provide as an objective assessment of how they can get better – as well as what they are already doing well – as opposed to a subjective riff on their deficits or lack of ability. Of course, we never intend our feedback to be the latter, but this alone does not stop some students perceiving it as such.

So what can we do to foster this culture of improvement, one in which all students see their learning as a work-in-progress, and feedback as a boon the teacher provides to help them develop? Here are five simple techniques you can call on:

1) Maintain the positive to critical ratio. We mentioned this earlier. For many students, giving multiple strengths and a target helps take the sting out of constructively critical comments. Done repeatedly, it habituates learners into a pattern: they know your feedback covers a number of things they've done well and only one thing they could improve. Avoid the trap of giving indiscriminate or meaningless praise, however. It is much more useful – in terms of developing student mindsets and helping them to understand what good looks like – if you ensure the strengths you identify are relevant and justified.

2) Talk in terms of 'we'. As in 'What we need to do next to improve your work...' or 'I'd like to see you using a greater range of examples to show your wider understanding. We can work on this together next lesson.' This technique places you and the student on the same team. It is particularly useful when a student feels feedback is 'done to them' as it subtly withdraws this sense of a 'me and you' dynamic. You can also talk in terms of 'we' after students receive their written feedback. While the class are reading and acting on what you have written, identify those students who would most benefit from hearing this kind of language and go and talk to them about their feedback. Reframe what you have written in terms of 'we'. Draw students' attention to this and make explicit that you and they are on the same team and that you are working together to improve their work.

3) Give examples of what change will look like. This helps students visualise what their work will look like once they've implemented your targets. Some learners find it difficult to project forward in a positive manner. They don't necessarily believe they can improve and so struggle to take the information you are giving them, hold it in their minds and turn it into a potential future. Giving examples of what change will look like serves two purposes. First, it helps students understand why your feedback is relevant and how it can be of particular use to them. Second, it presents students with a model of implementation from which they can borrow – or which they can imitate – making acting on your feedback a little easier.

4) Refer to changes and improvements students have made in the past. Here we are invoking the existing experience students have of developing themselves and their learning. We are reminding them of the positive steps they have previously taken and may have forgotten – or deliberately overlooked. They can use this past experience as a means through which to engage with their current feedback. It is also a point of reference for the general benefits of acting on feedback. The argument being that they have done it before, reaped the rewards, and can thus do it again, reaping different rewards as a result.

5) Invite students to give written feedback. This can be in a number of forms: self-assessment, peer-assessment, assessment of a piece of exemplar work, assessment of your teaching or assessment of the lesson as a whole. In each case, the aim is to help students better understand the process of delivering written feedback so as to change how they perceive the written feedback you give to them. To successfully achieve this change, draw students' attention to what is happening as they give their feedback. Help them to understand that when we assess something we make judgements and that these judgements are about what we think does and does not accord with the criteria we invoke. And that those things in the latter category are the areas around which we build targets, so that improvements can be made. Doing this helps bring the structure and purpose of feedback out into the open. It removes much of the emotional content students may project onto it, effectively neutralising negative perceptions and making it easier for learners to act on constructive criticism.

What do you want students to do with your feedback?

Asking yourself this question means clarifying and refining the purpose of your marking. If you have a clear sense of what you want students to do with your written feedback, then it becomes easier to mark in a way which supports this purpose. Conversely, if you don't really have any idea of what you want students to do, then your marking will have less focus and your feedback may lack relevance.

To illustrate, consider two different teachers.

Teacher A knows what they want their students to do with their feedback. They want them to read it through when the books are returned, discuss it with a partner, then take their target and try to apply it during the next three lessons, after which, the teacher will take the books in again, mark them and see how successful students have been. They will then provide another round of written feedback.

Teacher B has a vague idea of what they want students to do with their feedback. Ideally, they would like them to understand it and to improve their work as a result. They hope this will happen and plan to check in a few lessons' time to see if it has.

There is not a huge amount of difference between the positions of Teacher A and Teacher B. The key difference, though, is in the level of control Teacher A is exerting over the process of providing feedback and ensuring students understand and act on it. Teacher B is more passive. Their intentions are good but they are leaving more to chance and good fortune than Teacher A.

Teacher A sees their written feedback as part of a wider process. One which includes comprehension, reflection, analysis and action on the part of the students. They mark in accordance with this view. Their intention is to provide information which students will use in specific ways, in the lesson, under the guiding hand of the teacher. There is still an expectation that students will work independently and take ownership of their feedback, but Teacher A intends to set up a structure which facilitates this and has a clear idea about how they will follow up and judge success.

Thinking about what you want students to do with your written feedback means thinking about the impact you want that feedback to have and what you can do to ensure this happens. It means your marking is underpinned by a sense of purpose. One which drives your engagement with students' work and subsequently drives their engagement with your feedback.

To help you think about what you want students to do with your feedback, here are some examples you can use or adapt:

- Try to implement it for homework and bring the results to the next lesson.

- Use it to make immediate changes to what you are doing.

- Use it to improve an ongoing project.

- Identify how you can use it to improve your most recent piece of work.

- Redo a section of the work I've marked, taking account of your feedback.

- Reflect on it, thinking about what you wanted to achieve, what you did achieve and why this happened.

- Use it to change how you engage with the learning.

- Use it to think differently about the topic.

- Adjust your efforts based on the information I've provided.

- Identify where the strengths I've identified can be found in your work – as well as the area for improvement I've picked out.

In each example written feedback becomes part of a wider process. The teacher marks students' work with the expectation that their feedback will be used in a certain way. They set up situations to facilitate this – either in lessons or, as in the first example, outside of lessons.

Planning for Students to Respond and Reflect

Let us develop a little further this theme of planning how students interact with your feedback. When delivering verbal feedback, students normally respond in the moment – directly after we have spoken to them. This might be with questions or comments of their own. Or it might be by making changes to what they are doing.

Written feedback differs for two reasons. First, it tends to be more complex, detailed or both. This is because we have spent longer thinking about student work and synthesising our understanding of it to create relevant feedback giving useful access to our expertise. Second, students need more time to decode, interpret and make sense of the feedback we provide. When we give verbal feedback we accompany this with gestures, intonation and other non-verbal cues. This is supplementary information students can use to understand what is going on. When we give written feedback, none of this is present – just the words on the page. So students tend to need that bit more time in which to make sense of it.

Planning for students to respond and reflect is similar to using wait time when posing questions. This is where we pose a question to an individual student, a group or the whole class and then wait...before taking any answers. The purpose of the wait time is to let students think about the question so they can give a more thoughtful answer. This is different to posing a question and demanding an answer immediately, which often leads to lower quality answers, 'I don't know' or a refusal to answer.

Planning time in which students can respond to and reflect on our feedback means making sure there is time in which they can think about what we have written. The principle is the same as wait time. Students need space so they can make sense of what is going on – of the information contained in our feedback. If we don't provide this space, they will probably forget about our feedback or fail to tell us if they don't understand it or don't know how they are meant to act on it.

There are many ways in which you can plan for student responses and reflection. Here are seven examples:

- Turn your starter activity into a period of reflection during which students review your feedback and think about how they can use it to improve their work.

- Plan a mid-lesson review in which you lead students in a reflection on their most recent piece of written feedback. Encourage them to think about this in light of what they are doing in the current lesson.

- Create a timetable for marking student books and use this to build time into your lessons when responding to and reflecting on feedback is the main focus. By planning ahead you can see when you will be returning student books and therefore when it will be most appropriate to include this time.

- Use a plenary to help students reflect on their most recent piece of written feedback. Focus their attention on how the feedback connects to the lesson just gone. For example, can they see evidence of the strengths you identified in the work they've been doing?

- Create a system for responding to and reflecting on feedback. For example, you might explain to students that whenever they get their work back after you've marked it, there will automatically be a ten minute hiatus during which everybody reflects and responds. Scaffold this with questions students can use to structure their thinking.

- Identify specific students who will benefit from one-to-one support. After you hand back work containing written feedback, either call these students to the front or visit them at their desks during the course of the lesson. Use this as an opportunity to talk to them about their feedback.

Use questioning, suggestions and prompts to scaffold their responses and reflections.

- Create a space in which students can write responses to or reflections on your feedback. For example, you might draw a box underneath your written comments and invite students to fill this in. Or, you might create a pro-forma containing space for your feedback and space in which students can write their responses and reflections.

In the next chapter we'll look at strategies where the focus is solely on students responding to and implementing their targets. You can consider those as an adjunct to this list.

Focussing on Mistakes

One area on which you might like to focus your written feedback is mistakes. This can take two forms: praising students and suggesting where improvements might lie. In the first case, we can give praise by highlighting how students have learned from their mistakes and by indicating that this is a strength of their work. We can also praise students for making mistakes when these mistakes are a result of embracing challenges, intellectual risk-taking and pushing themselves. Or, we can praise students for using trial and error as a tool through which to learn – with this inevitably including the making of mistakes.

In the second case, we can identify mistakes students are making and use these as the basis of the targets we suggest, or we can indicate that these are the areas on which students should focus if they want to improve their work. We are using mistakes as a signal that the work is challenging. And we are providing students with access to the area of our expertise which will help them go beyond what they can presently do.

If you decide to focus your written feedback on mistakes – in part or in full – it is worth doing some preparatory work with students so they understood what is happening and why you are doing it. Three steps I would suggest are as follows:

1) Talk to students about the relationship between mistake-making and being challenged. Help them to understand that mistakes are not a bad thing but very often a sign that the level of challenge is sufficiently high. Give examples to illustrate this, including from your own experience. Explain to students that trial and error is an important way in which we learn and that this is predicated on making mistakes and learning from these.

2) Distinguish between careless and useful mistakes. Careless mistakes are those mistakes which students could have avoided if they had been paying more attention. They are the result of inattentiveness, rushing or a lack of focus and are not indicative of any wider lack of understanding. Useful mistakes, on the other hand, give access to information we can learn from, and which we can use to avoid making similar mistakes in the future. For example, a misplaced comma is often a careless mistake, whereas incorrect use of a newly learned word is a useful mistake – because it helps us to better understand the meaning of that word and how to use it correctly.

3) Model for students how to make good use of mistake-based feedback. This has two parts to it. First, you need to help students understand that such feedback is essentially neutral or positive – it does not have a negative content. Many learners struggle with this because they see mistakes as a problem – something to avoid rather than embrace. You need to disabuse them of this idea. Case studies, examples and exemplar work demonstrating how mistaking-making can lead to swift progress are all good tools to call on. Second, show students how they can take your feedback and apply it. For example, you might show them how to identify warning signs indicating they are about to make a similar mistake as before. Or, you might give them a checklist they can use to identify when a similar mistake crops up – meaning they are then in a position to do something about it.

Focussing your written feedback on mistakes means helping students to see mistake-making as a useful part of the learning process. It also means your marking has a clear focus – the identification, highlighting and correction of mistakes (though you might leave the latter up to students) combined with provision of mistake-based feedback. If used repeatedly, this can help give your written feedback a greater sense of coherence. Students come to expect that the information you convey will focus on the mistakes they've made and the learning they've done in response to previous mistakes. This forms a virtuous circle as students respond to your feedback, correcting, learning from and avoiding mistakes, only to make new ones as the level of challenge increases. You then give new feedback on these mistakes and the process continues.

Highlighting Specific Areas

We conclude the chapter with a technique you can use to help students focus their efforts on a specific aspect of their work. The idea is to maximise the return the student sees on their investment. By focussing on one particular thing, they can bring about fairly major changes in a short space of time. Here's how it works:

When you are marking student work, select one specific aspect of what they have done and highlight this. The easiest way is to draw a box around it using a coloured pen. Another option is to use a highlighter.

Next, write your feedback in the nearest possible place, making sure that it is exclusively focussed on the area you have highlighted. This means you are not providing feedback in the form of an overview covering all elements of the student's work. Instead, you are providing highly focussed feedback dealing with one aspect of their work.

When you return work to your students, explain what you have done. Indicate that your aim is to help them make quick improvements in a specific area, rather than asking them to think about their work as a whole. Give them time to respond and reflect on your feedback. Circulate through the room and offer support to students who need it.

You now have two options. First, you can set a time limit and ask students to act on your feedback immediately by redoing the part of their work you have highlighted. Second, you can tell students when they will next have a chance to act on your feedback. For example, in the last section of the lesson. They should ready themselves to act on it at that point. Either way, you are making sure you close the gap. This means the process runs as follows:

- Students produce work.

- Teacher marks work.

- Teacher picks out a specific section of the work, highlights this and gives feedback.

- Students read, respond and reflect on feedback.

- Students act on feedback – either immediately or soon after.

In certain cases, this is a highly effective structure on which to draw. For example, students might be working on coursework or a controlled assessment. In these situations, specific, targeted feedback will help them to quickly improve a key aspect of their work. Another example is project-based work, where the provision of focused feedback followed by an immediate opportunity to implement it can help students improve the overall quality of what they are doing before they move on. The approach can also eliminate the risk of students compounding any errors they are making.

You can develop the technique by challenging students to tell you in advance what specific areas of their work they think you should highlight and give feedback on. This puts the onus on them to carefully assess their own efforts and break their work down into a series of separate elements. Or, to put it another way, to analyse their work in a manner similar to that employed by the teacher.

Chapter Six – Targets and Target Implementation

Setting Targets

What do you want targets to do?

This question is our starting point for a discussion around targets. What do you want targets to do? Answering this question means gaining a better understanding of why you are setting targets and how you expect students to use them, as well as what change you hope to effect through the provision of your targets. It may not take you long to answer, but it is worth attending to. Without a clear understanding of why you are setting targets and a vision for what you want them to achieve, there is a risk that you will fall into a routine in which targets become a token part of the process without a wider rationale underpinning their use.

This is not to say that targets won't have a positive impact in these circumstances. They may well do. But, I would argue, your actions inside the classroom and also while you are planning and marking, are likely to be better directed and more in line with your aims if you have a sound rationale supporting them.

For example, an art teacher might decide that they want their targets to consistently challenge students to improve the quality of their work. This sounds like an obvious point, but there are other options available: targets which effect a different way of looking, targets which encourage revision and reflection, targets based on metacognition. Having a precise meaning animating target-setting means marking and giving feedback through a lens which you have chosen.

In the example, our art teacher will question whether students have been sufficiently challenged as they assess their work, and use the answers they derive from this to inform their subsequent target-setting. Over time, this will lead to targets being set which accord with the teacher's intentions. If you lack clarity of understanding regarding what you are trying to achieve through your targets, you will arguably be much less likely to achieve what you want.

So spend a few minutes asking yourself why you are setting targets and what you hope to achieve by doing this. Then use your answers to inform your marking and feedback.

Of course, there are many reasons why you might set targets, all of them equally valid. And there is nothing stopping you switching between them, or even deciding to rank two or three as being of equal importance. With that in mind, here are seven key areas you might choose to focus on:

- **Active Practice.** This is practice in which the student is actively engaged. It differs from passive practice where the student is repeating a process without fully attending to what they are doing. Targets focused on active practice ask students to repeat something while thinking carefully about it. They must fully engage with the act of practice. This leads to more sustained improvement than would otherwise be the case.

For example, a PE teacher might set the following target: 'I want you to focus on watching the ball onto the bat. Follow it with your eyes from the bowler's hand until it hits the bat. Think about what you're doing as you practice.' Here the teacher gives advice about how the student can improve their technique. They inculcate an element of active practice by asking the student to attend to what they are doing while they are trying to do it. The focus is on both implementation of a change in process and active engagement with the attempt to make that change.

This principle can be applied in all areas of the curriculum. It can overlap with some of the other options detailed below, or remain your sole focus. It can be particularly useful if you feel students' efforts aren't leading to the results you expect. Or if students are claiming they see no point in repetition. In these cases, focussing on active practice means channelling student effort so that more tangible results are produced; and so the impact of practice is both greater and easier for students to see.

- **Editing, Rewriting, Redoing.** Many students like to finish a piece of work and then move on. Many do not like being asked to edit, rewrite or redo some or all of what they have done. They often see this as a futile endeavour, or feel that the teacher is making unfair demands on them. In the minds of these students, the work is done when it is done.

We know that sometimes this is the case, but that often it isn't. Often there is room for improvement and students will benefit from going back and reviewing what they've produced. We recognise the benefits of seeing work as a work-in-progress, and seeing an end product as something a little further off; not something necessarily achieved on immediate completion of a task.

Focussing your targets on editing, rewriting and redoing encourages students to change how they view their work and to improve the quality of what they produce.

If taking this route, which has much to recommend it, it is worth spending a bit of time explaining to students why these processes are worth doing and how a piece of work is likely to improve as a result of being edited, rewritten or redone. The purpose is to help them better understand what revision and amendment can lead to. Through doing this groundwork you make it more likely that students will respond positively to the nature of your targets; hopefully embracing them but, if not, at least appreciating their utility.

- **Changing Processes.** Processes are what produce work and underpin learning. They are open to change and, as we saw above in the example of the PE teacher, are a prime area on which to focus your targets. When it comes to changing processes, targets are often about the teacher giving access to their expert knowledge of how a process can work more effectively. The aim is to transfer this expertise from the teacher's mind to the student's mind, so that the student can alter the processes they are using when producing work.

For example, an English teacher might identify a learner who is tending to write in a stream of consciousness style, instead of refining and editing their thinking before committing it to paper. They might then use their expertise to set a target such as: 'I'd like you to think through your thoughts first, speak them aloud and then pare them down so they express your ideas more clearly and succinctly. Then put them in a written sentence.'

This target is essentially a stepping stone helping the student to take a first step in changing the process of sentence construction they are currently using. We can imagine the teacher helping the student to build on this with further targets later down the line. The teacher's aim would be to help the student significantly improve their process of constructing written sentences over time, aware that this needs to be done gradually and cannot be achieved all at once.

- **Securing Knowledge.** Secure knowledge is an absolute necessity for successful learning, so it is natural that there will be times when you decide to focus your targets on this. In these situations, it is often about helping learners to improve the depth, range and accuracy of their knowledge. Frequently this entails asking them to revisit things they have already studied, with a view to gaining a sounder understanding. However, it can also mean focussing on mistakes and misconceptions students are making – either because of their insecure knowledge or due to them applying knowledge inexpertly.

For example, a science teacher might set a target such as the following: 'Compare how you have answered the question with the model answer. Look at the greater amount of scientific knowledge included in the model. I'd like you to go back to your notes and identify which areas are lacking in detail. You can then improve these.' Here the emphasis is on helping the student to understand that their performance in the task (answering the question) is directly related to the knowledge they currently possess. The target directs the student to develop and finesse that knowledge.

It is often useful to suggest different techniques students can use to secure their knowledge. For example: practice testing; synthesising knowledge into new forms; application of knowledge to tasks or questions; creation of mind-maps; teaching of knowledge to a peer or parent. All these techniques offer students active ways in which they can revisit, develop and enhance their existing knowledge. In the process they help to secure a broader and more nuanced level of understanding.

- **Increasing the Level of Challenge.** You might decide to focus your targets on increasing the level of challenge. This involves assessing the extent to which students have been challenged by the tasks you've set. As you mark student work, you will be asking yourself whether students have been pushed to the edge of what they can do without support – and whether they have had their thinking, skills or abilities stretched beyond what they can do comfortably.

Setting targets based on this information means first deciding how challenged students have been and then deciding whether a sufficient level of challenge will come from a target connected to their existing work or something which goes beyond this.

For example, a maths teacher might be marking student work and identify two different students, one who is challenged by the current tasks and one who is clearly finding them too easy. In the case of the former, a challenging target does not need to introduce anything new. The level of challenge can be increased simply by asking the student to persist with the current work and to perhaps think about some additional aspect of it. In the latter case, the student needs a target which goes beyond what the class are presently doing. This illustrates how assessment of current levels of challenge informs what a challenging target looks like.

You might also decide to increase the level of challenge by asking students to identify where and when the work has been too easy for them. You can then use this information to inform target-setting. This sees you inviting students into the process of assessing the right level of challenge; something which promotes independence and also encourages them to see high challenge in a positive light. Something to strive for, rather than avoid.

- **Broadening Student Thinking.** This is our penultimate suggestion for a target-setting rationale. Perhaps you will decide that the aim of your targets is to broaden student thinking. This could be an aim which remains dominant throughout the year, or something you turn to at certain points, such as the beginning of a new topic. Either way, the type of targets you set will alter as a result of your choice. This again demonstrates the subtle but significant impact defining the purpose of your target-setting can have on the feedback students receive and, by extension, the way in which they focus their efforts.

Here are a selection of targets informed by the desire to broaden student thinking:

i) (Literacy) 'I'd like you to try reading a book from a different genre. Choose something you don't normally read. Tell me what you think about your choice and we'll talk about how you could use some of the ideas in your own writing.'

ii) (Geography) 'Pick a European country you know very little about. Research the country and see how its economic, geographic and demographic landscape is similar and different to the UK. Then tell me how your research could inform your future work.'

iii) (Primary Science) 'Pick a material from the list. Choose something you don't know much about. Then, team up with someone who chose the same material. Your target is to become experts in this – and to be ready to tell the rest of the class all about it.'

In each case, the teacher is using targets to push student thinking – either beyond the boundaries of the lesson, or beyond the boundaries of the familiar.

- Promoting Independence. The final suggestion for a rationale to underpin target-setting is the promotion of independence. If this is the animating purpose guiding your targets then you will be thinking about how your feedback can help students take greater ownership of their work and their learning. This might be something which is appropriate to all students in your class, or it might be relevant to a select few. For example, you might identify a group of learners who struggle to pull themselves out of a passive relationship with their learning. These learners tend to believe they are not in control of their own destinies and therefore that their efforts do not influence how successful they are.

Targets which promote independence are often about helping students adopt new ways of thinking or working. The aim is to shift their outlook from passive to active. That is, one in which their own decisions determine what happens with their learning. One in which they understand and believe in their own sense of agency.

Here are three examples:

- 'When you find the work challenging, I would like you to try adopting a different strategy. See if this works and, if it doesn't, try to work out why.

If you're still having difficulties, then let me know. We can discuss what you tried and look for an alternative together.'

- 'I'd like to see you using more trial and error in your work. Instead of giving up when you think you can't be successful, try something out. Don't worry if it goes wrong. Have a go, think about what happened and then see what you can learn from it.'

- 'Make sure you try three different things before asking me for help. Think about the problem yourself, then consult a book, then ask a peer for their advice. If you're still stuck, talk to me about it. If you aren't, then you've solved the problem yourself!'

In each of these examples, notice how the target encourages students to see themselves as the primary movers in their own learning. The implicit message is that success is more likely to arrive through persistence and taking control than through giving up or resigning oneself to a belief that nothing can change.

These set of exemplar rationales is not comprehensive, but it does cover a number of key bases and give a sense of the kind of impact having an underpinning purpose can have. You can pick and choose from what I've exemplified, identify your own, or modify any of the above. Whatever you choose to do, remember the central message is that having a purpose clarifies what you are doing and why you are doing it, increasing the efficacy of your work.

For more on targets and target-setting, see Chapter Ten, where you will find 150 exemplar targets. The next thing we need to think about here, though, is target implementation. Without this, it is likely your targets will not have the impact on student learning you desire. In fact, they might not have any impact at all.

Target Implementation

Planning for Target Implementation

Students need time in which to implement their targets. Without this the targets may well disappear into the ether, never to be effectively acted upon. While some conscientious learners can be relied on to implement their targets without additional support or specific time in which to do so, many students do not have the skills or disposition to do this.

The problem is particularly acute when the demands of the curriculum encourage the teacher to move from unit to unit without affording time for reflection or target implementation. A common scenario sees books being marked at the end of a unit, returned at the start of the next, replete with feedback, and the teacher then starting the new unit without giving students any dedicated time in which to act on the feedback they've received.

In the remainder of this chapter, we will look at five techniques you can use to help students implement their targets and think carefully about the feedback they receive. All the techniques are linked by the same premise: that the teacher should consider how and when students will have an opportunity to implement their targets and that this should inform their planning. Each technique is exemplified through classroom examples.

In addition to the techniques below, you might also like to think about other ways in which you can weave target implementation into lessons. For example, by circulating through the class during activities and reminding students of their targets. Or, by planning lessons in which you work intensively with small groups of students, helping them to implement their targets while the rest of the class work independently – either on their targets or on another task or activity.

D.I.R.T.

This stands for Directed Improvement and Reflection Time. It simply means the teacher sets aside a period of time in which everyone's focus is on reviewing feedback, reflecting on feedback and trying to implement feedback. For example, a primary school teacher might decide to have D.I.R.T. once a day for twenty minutes. This time would then have a red box around it in the teacher's planning, making it sacrosanct.

Every iteration would see the teacher and their learners focussing on reviewing, reflecting on and implementing feedback. The teacher might circulate during this time, offering support to different students. Or, they might work closely with one or two learners, helping them to understand what their targets mean and how to make effective changes in their work. Another option would see the teacher working closely with a small group of learners who have all received feedback of a similar type.

However D.I.R.T. is used, it ensures that dedicated time is provided during which feedback and targets are everyone's top priority. This stops targets getting lost, being forgotten or being ignored.

Example 1: An English teacher in a secondary school sees their Year 9 class four times a week. They decide to give over the first twenty minutes of every fourth lesson to D.I.R.T. During this time, no new content is taught. The only focus is on existing feedback and the targets students are trying to implement. The teacher explains what they are doing, and why, so that students are on board with the process. In addition, they decide in advance how their time will be best used – whether it involves circulating, scaffolding and modelling, or working with specific learners. This changes from week to week in line with the needs of the class. Over time, students come to expect D.I.R.T. every fourth lesson. They see it as part of their routine and, because of this, assume that reviewing, reflecting on and trying to implement targets is the norm – exactly what the teacher wants them to think.

Example 2: A PE teacher in a primary school turns the first ten minutes of their lessons over to D.I.R.T. Because they don't see their students that often, they don't always have time to give detailed individual feedback. To overcome this, they create a list of ten targets for each D.I.R.T. session. They print this off and bring it with them to the lesson. As soon as D.I.R.T. begins, the teacher brings out their target list and invites learners to select one target from it which they will then focus on trying to implement in the first ten minutes of the session. The target lists are informed by the work students have been doing in previous lessons, as well as the longer term progress they are making. This way, the teacher knows that each list has something for everybody. While students are trying to implement their chosen targets, the teacher moves around, offering advice and further feedback. As with the previous example, students get used to this over time, until they expect it to happen and therefore see it as the norm.

Target Trackers

Take an A4 sheet of paper and divide it into three columns. At the top of the first column write 'Date' at the top of the second write 'Target' and at the top of the third write 'Date Achieved'. You now have a target tracker. It's as simple as that.

Stick this sheet in the front of students' books and you and they have an effective means through which to keep track of their targets. This avoids the risk that targets get lost as time progresses; superseded by the next piece of work, the one after that and so on. It also makes it easier for you to redirect students towards their targets. For example, you might ask them at the start of a lesson to take a look at their target trackers and, once reminded of these, to focus their energies accordingly.

Another option is to ask students to check their target trackers midway through a lesson. For example, you might get to the main task and then say: 'Just take a moment to have a look at your target tracker. What's your current target? How do you think you could work towards that during this activity?'

There's no great innovation here. It's just a simple system through which to keep tabs on targets. One which makes referencing them easy and straightforward.

An added benefit comes from the 'Date Achieved' column. By including this you indicate to students that the implementation of targets is an ongoing process. Something they should be working towards. And something that you will be looking to check up on. In terms of your planning, this can manifest itself as lesson segments during which you circulate through the room and ask students to show you how close they are to meeting their targets. You can then sign off where and when this is appropriate. Another possibility is to use the target tracker sheets to focus your marking. As you read through student work, do so with their current targets in mind. If you feel they have met or surpassed these, sign off the tracker sheet. If not, tailor your feedback in light of this and give them additional guidance on how to effectively meet their current target.

Example 1: A history teacher gives all their students a target tracker. They use this to record the targets they receive. The teacher plans to take students back to their target trackers at the start of every lesson. How they do this varies. In some lessons, they simply ask students to remind themselves of their current target and to think about how they might work on this in the session ahead. In other lessons, they explain to students what activities are to follow and ask them to discuss with a partner how these activities might give them good opportunities to implement their targets. And in still other lessons, the teacher turns the starter into a reflection activity during which students review their target trackers and discuss with a partner what they have achieved, how they have done this, where they are going and what they need to do next.

Example 2: A primary science teacher gives all their students a target tracker. When planning, they identify specific lessons during which students will have opportunities to work on their targets. In these lessons, the teacher asks learners to review their tracker sheets at the start of the session. During the lesson, they prompt learners to go back to their trackers and remind themselves of their targets. They also ask learners to then make a judgement about how successfully they are currently implementing their targets. Finally, they lead the class in a plenary at the end of the session during which reflection on target implementation – and the tracker sheets – is everyone's focus.

Activity-Based Implementation

Why not structure your planning so that students have the chance to implement their targets during the following lesson, and to do so through an appropriate activity? For example, a graphic design teacher might give their students feedback on the task of following a design brief. Each student would receive a target, and the teacher would then plan a lesson in which students receive a new brief to work on, while also trying to implement their targets.

This is the essence of activity-based implementation:

1) Students produce a piece of work.

2) Teacher gives feedback on this work.

3) Teacher plans a lesson in which the main focus is an activity through which students can implement their targets.

4) Students receive their feedback, review their targets, and try to implement them in the main activity.

You can use it in nearly any context, and it ensures students have an immediate opportunity to act on their feedback. This keeps targets fresh in their minds, avoids feedback disappearing into the ether and also allows for active engagement with the process of trying to improve your approach to a given piece of work.

The only downside of activity-based implementation is that you do need to think ahead. This means planning fairly well in advance for the four-step process outlined above. While this isn't onerous, it does mean you need to be on the ball, otherwise you might find yourself struggling to plan an appropriate activity (step 3) through which students can implement their targets. With that said, it is a drawback easily overcome. And one that often dissipates of its own accord once you are familiar with the technique.

Example 1: A religious studies teacher takes in a set of essays students have written about the relationship between religion and science. They mark these and then plan a lesson in which students have a new essay to write, focussing on the relationship between religion and politics. The work is returned to students at the start of the session. The teacher gives time for learners to review their feedback and think about what their targets mean. Then, they lead a whole-class discussion briefly examining how best to implement targets when writing essays. The remainder of the lesson sees students researching, planning and writing their essays – all the time thinking about their targets and how they can change their approach (compared to last time) so as to implement these.

Example 2: An economics teacher sets students a series of exam questions to answer. They take these in, mark them and then plan a lesson in which students have to work through a set of similar questions, but focussing on different content. The marked work is returned to students, who read through their feedback and discuss it with a partner. The teacher then invites students to interview two further peers and to ask them what feedback they received, what their target suggests about their most recent efforts, and how they think they can best act on this. It is a process which helps all students to articulate, edit and refine their thinking. The lesson then moves on, with the teacher introducing the new exam-style questions and inviting students to attempt these while also trying to implement their targets.

Modelling and Scaffolding Target Implementation

Sometimes, students will really struggle to implement your targets. They may not understand them, may find the process of change difficult or may find it hard to visualise how their work will be different from its current form. In these situations, it is worth using modelling and scaffolding as tools through which to make life that little bit easier for students.

Modelling target implementation can take many forms. These include:

- Physically showing a student how to implement a target. For example, an art teacher might show a student how they are currently applying colour and how they will apply colour in the future, if they successfully implement their target.

- Creating a piece of exemplar work. For example, a French teacher might create a piece of writing illustrating successful implementation of the student's target.

- Talking students through a new process. For example, a maths teacher might talk a student through the current (incorrect) way of thinking under which they are labouring before talking them through the correct way – which they will achieve upon implementing their target.

In each case, we see the teacher modelling successful target implementation for the student. This makes life easier for them. They now know what they are aiming for – and they have a model from which they can borrow or which they can imitate.

Scaffolding target implementation can also take many forms. These include:

- Prompting the student to think about a particular approach. For example, a biology teacher might prompt a student to think about previous methods they have used to successfully implement targets.

- Giving clues about how successful target implementation might work. For example, a PE teacher might point to a student in the class who can already do what the learner is trying to achieve and invite them to observe and question their peer for clues about successful target implementation.

- Suggesting some different things for students to think about. For example, a citizenship teacher might suggest that a student thinks about how they want their speech to look, sound and feel to a variety of different audiences. These suggestions would tie directly to the target the student is trying to implement.

In each of these examples, the teacher gives students a little bit of support – a touch of scaffolding. This does some of the work for them, shuttling them gently in the right direction, before leaving the main effort up to them.

Demonstrating Competence

Our final technique connected to target implementation is demonstrating competence. This is where we give students opportunities to demonstrate competence to us, or one of their peers, during the course of a lesson. It means planning sessions in which these opportunities take centre stage, and making students aware of what is going on and why.

Demonstrating competence means showing that you have successfully implemented whatever target you were striving for. The competence concerns the learner's ability to successfully demonstrate their improved approach, knowledge, understanding or skill. For example, a textiles teacher might set a student the target of sewing with greater precision so as to give their finished work a more professional appearance. The teacher would then plan a lesson (or lessons) during which the student has a chance to work on this target before trying to demonstrate competence.

If the teacher is happy that the student has successfully demonstrated competence, that means they have implemented their target. They can then move onto a new target, based on a different element of the teacher's expertise. If, however, the teacher does not believe the student is demonstrating competence as yet, then they can use this as an opportunity to offer further help, support and guidance.

Planning lessons in this way means planning to get students' attempts at target implementation out into the open. Once they are there, it becomes quicker and easier to judge where students are at and to give feedback in response.

Example 1: A primary school teacher is teaching literacy. They have recently given learners feedback around writing to inform. Each learner has a target on which they are working. The teacher plans a series of three lessons. In the first two, learners have ample opportunity to practice implementing their targets. In the third lesson, demonstrating competence becomes the focus. Here, the teacher wants to assess, during the session, which students have successfully implemented their targets and which are yet to do so. They can then give appropriate feedback and support in response.

Example 2: A philosophy teacher gives their students feedback on how to argue more effectively. Every student in the class has a target. The teacher plans a series of activities over the next two lessons during which students have a chance to implement their targets in a variety of different settings. On top of this, they plan opportunities for reflection during which students can think about how successful they have been, discuss what strengths and weaknesses they have shown and decide how to move forward. At the end of the second lesson, the teacher sets an essay. Students must complete this for homework and, so the teacher indicates, attempt to demonstrate competence regarding their target as part of the process.

Chapter Seven – Further Feedback Techniques

Introduction

In this chapter we examine a selection of feedback techniques not mentioned elsewhere. The purpose is to provide further strategies on which you can draw to maximise the effectiveness and impact of your feedback. Each technique is explained and then exemplified through two different areas of the curriculum. This helps to provide context and demonstrate how you might choose to apply the technique. The chapter builds on points made earlier in the book – especially those contained in Chapters One and Two. These won't be repeated here, but they are implicit in what follows.

Whole-Class Feedback Lists

These can save you a lot of time while also providing personalised feedback to all the students in your class. Having marked a set of books, instead of writing formative feedback in those books, turn the various comments you would have provided into a list of targets. This list should encompass all the students in your class – every student should be able to pick out at least one item on the list and see it as relevant to them and their work.

Next lesson, return student books and display the list on the board. Explain that you have marked students' work and that this list is a synthesis of your feedback. It contains all the comments you feel are appropriate to the class as a whole. Invite students to read through the list, to look at their own work and to identify which target is most appropriate for them. As this is happening, circulate through the room so you can observe which targets students are choosing. If a student chooses an inappropriate target, or one which is too easy or too hard, then advise them to select a different one.

When all students have identified a suitable target, provide some time in which they can act on these – by redoing a section of their work, for example. This is again a good opportunity to circulate. You can offer students support and guidance, pose questions which stretch their thinking and model successful target implementation for them.

Example 1: Literacy. The teacher marks a set of books and then creates the following list, which they display on the board at the start of the next lesson, as they hand the books back:

1. Decrease the length of your sentences.

2. Look up spellings you're not sure of.

3. Use punctuation to break up longer sentences.

4. Make sure you stay in the same tense.

5. Look for different ways to start your sentences – don't always use 'I'.

6. If you start writing in the 3rd person, continue writing in the 3rd person.

7. Include more detail in your writing – try describing more things.

8. Use a thesaurus to select a wider variety of words.

9. Make sure you always write in sentences.

10. Look at where you have used capital letters. What could you change?

Students are given a chance to look through their books. The teacher then invites them to examine the list and decide which target is most relevant to them. If more than one target is relevant, the teacher asks students to select the one they think is most important. Time is then provided in which students can act on their targets. The teacher circulates, offering support.

There are a couple of variations we can mention here. First, the teacher might decide not to circulate. Instead, they could identify in advance a handful of students they feel will benefit from one-to-one support. They would then use the target implementation time to support these learners. Second, instead of leaving it to students to select a target, they could write a number in students' books, with this number corresponding to the target on the list which is appropriate for them. In this formulation, the teacher reads through the books, creates the list, then goes back and writes a number at the end of each student's piece of work.

Example 2: Geography. The teacher marks a set of assignments, produces the following list and displays it on the board as they return work to students:

1. Use specific examples to illustrate your points. Help the reader understand why your argument is persuasive.

2. Evaluate the arguments you use. Identify their strengths and weaknesses – or use different arguments to critique each other.

3. Go into more detail in your work. Explain your ideas in full – imagine that the reader has no clue about the topic and needs you to help them out.

4. Avoid slang language and include more technical language. Try to write like a geographer, using the language of geography. Focus on using the terminology we've been learning.

5. Compare different ideas in your work. Show the similarities and differences between them. This helps demonstrate your ability to analyse key information.

The list is shorter than in the literacy example because the nature of the assignment means students are making similar errors across the board. The teacher uses the list as a tool to not only help students improve the quality of their work in a general sense, but also as a way to help them draw it closer to the demands of the mark-scheme. As part of this, they share the mark-scheme with students and explain how the different targets relate to different sections, as well as how they are indicative of good geographical work more widely. This approach helps students to better understand why they should improve their work and what impact implementing their target is likely to have.

Mistake Crib Sheets

Mistakes are an integral part of learning. They give access to information we can use to change future efforts. Trial and error is built on the premise that we learn from the mistakes we make – and then act on this learning in subsequent trials. When students make mistakes, we are in a position to give them useful feedback. This feedback usually focuses on why the mistake was made and how to avoid repeating it. We are helping students understand the cause of their mistake and the learning they can derive from this.

Mistake crib sheets are a different way through which to give feedback of this type. Instead of waiting for students to make mistakes, we share with them in advance the mistakes they are likely to make – or the mistakes which regularly crop up in a given topic.

A mistake crib sheet brings together the common errors and misconceptions students make when learning a topic. We use our prior experience to construct the crib sheet. Unlike our students, we have this experience on which to call. While they are encountering the topic for the first time, we are teaching it for perhaps the fifth or sixth time. Over the course of our previous endeavours, we have seen students making certain mistakes and labouring under certain misconceptions.

We collate this information into a crib sheet and share it with our current students. This is a form of pre-emptive feedback. We are saying to our learners:

- Everyone makes mistakes, they are nothing to worry about.

- Mistakes are a standard part of learning.

- Here are some of the mistakes I've seen students make in the past, and why they've made them.

- Use the crib sheet to help you. If you make a mistake, consult the sheet and see what you can learn.

- Look out for possible mistakes on the horizon. Familiarise yourself with the crib sheet and be ready to spot mistakes or misconceptions in your own work.

When handing out the crib sheets for the first time, talk students through them. Use your explanation to highlight the nature of the mistakes you have collated – why they are mistakes, where they arise from, what can be learned from them – as well as the different ways in which students can use the crib sheets – as a tool for analysing their own work, as an aide memoire, and as a primer for better understanding the topic.

Finally, encourage students to refer back to the crib sheets through the course of the topic. Promote this by having your own mistake crib sheet on hand. You can then model the use of this during activities and at the start and end of lessons. In so doing, you will help students to understand how they can use their copies and why doing this is beneficial.

Example 1: PE. The teacher is delivering a unit of work focussing on throwing in athletics. Students are trying out discus, javelin and shot. The teacher has made a mistake crib sheet for each one. They have blown this up onto A3 paper, laminated it and placed three copies next to each of the throwing areas. As the teacher takes students through each discipline, they encourage them to look at the mistake crib sheets and see some of the errors they are likely to make as they try to master the respective techniques. The teacher explains why these errors occur, what impact they are likely to have on throwing distances and how to avoid them.

The crib sheets are left out so that students can refer to them while they are practising. A nice development sees peer-assessment brought in. One student picks up a mistake crib sheet and refers to this as they watch their peer attempt a throw. They then give that peer feedback, using the crib sheet as a point of reference. This increases the quality of the feedback and means the peer who is being assessed can feel confident that the advice they are getting is connected to the initial analysis conducted by the teacher (which was formalised in the crib sheet).

Example 2: Biology. The teacher creates a crib sheet covering common mistakes and misconceptions students make when studying genetics at Key Stage 3. They use a mixture of text and images and divide the sheet in half so that each mistake or misconception is mirrored by a correct answer, approach or way of thinking. This results in a crib sheet with mistakes and misconceptions down the left hand side and the corresponding correct approaches down the right hand side.

The teacher hands this out at the start of the unit and gives students time to discuss it in pairs. They pose a few questions to facilitate this, including 'Are any of the mistakes or misconceptions ones you think you are already making?' Next, they lead a whole class discussion. First students share their thoughts. Then, the teacher talks through some or all of the items on the crib sheet. As they do, they draw students' attention to the key differences between the left and right hand sides. This process is all about helping students to understand in advance how key areas of the topic work and why mistakes or misconceptions around these are likely to occur. It works by giving students direct access to the teacher's expertise. Finally, the teacher asks students to keep the crib sheets to hand, ready for use through the rest of the topic.

Pre-Emptive Feedback

I would wager that in the vast majority of activities you know in advance the vast majority of the feedback you are likely to give. This is because you are the expert and you are in possession of a large stock of knowledge regarding the topic you are teaching. In all cases, except that of the beginning teacher, this stock includes knowledge of what students have done previously when completing activities of this type.

Pre-emptive feedback sees you tapping into your expertise and prior knowledge so as to outline in advance some of the key ways in which students can improve their work. Let's illustrate this with an example.

In an English lesson, the teacher has planned an activity in which students are asked to create a piece of persuasive writing. Having used a similar task before, and being experienced in the teaching of persuasive writing, the teacher is well placed to accurately predict the kind of mistakes students will make, the kind of things they will overlook, and the kind of things they will ignore or fail to do. This means the teacher is in a great position from which to craft pre-emptive feedback. That is, feedback which closely matches students' needs, even though it has been crafted prior to their completing the work in question.

Imagine our English teacher sitting down in advance of the lesson. They run through their plan and then focus on the persuasive writing activity. Calling on their expertise and prior experience, they identify five key pieces of feedback they feel will cover most students in the class. They add a slide into their PowerPoint detailing this feedback. In the lesson proper, they reveal this slide when students are about two-thirds of the way through the persuasive writing activity. Suddenly, every student in the class has something they can focus on to improve their work. And, if any students are not covered by the pre-emptive feedback, the teacher can work with these students directly during the last third of the activity, giving them personalised feedback on which to act.

Repeated use of the technique habituates students into an expectation that the work they produce during activities is a work-in-progress rather than a finished product. This helps them to see their efforts as being open to change and leads them to expect feedback as standard – something which the teacher provides automatically, with a view to helping students improve, even as they are doing something for the first time.

Example 1: History. The teacher has planned a lesson in which students examine a variety of sources from World War One, all of which come from the very start of the war. The overarching objective is to help students develop a sense of the different attitudes prevalent at the time and to encourage a critical engagement with a range of sources. Having taught the topic previously, the teacher knows that the first half of this activity is mostly taken up by students examining the sources, decoding them, assimilating them and clarifying their meaning. With this in mind, they prepare pre-emptive feedback focussing on the second part of their objective – encouraging a critical engagement with the sources. They prepare the following five targets as pre-emptive feedback, which they intend to reveal when the activity is about half-way through:

1. Contrast two of the sources. Focus on identifying the similarities and differences in the attitudes to which they give access.

2. Consider the extent to which the attitudes revealed by the sources are likely to be true. Analyse where the sources come from and use this to gauge how reliable they are.

3. Try to explain why different attitudes are present in the sources. Think about the views of the authors, as well as their previous experiences.

4. Evaluate the usefulness of the sources in explaining general attitudes to the war. Consider whose voices are absent as well as whose voices we can gain access to.

5. Use one of the sources to critique the others. Look at the other sources through the lens of your chosen one. Identify how that particular source can shed light on the others.

Notice how this feedback directs students towards more complex cognitive processes. It is likely, given the shape of the activity, that many of them will not have started thinking in these ways by the midpoint of the task. The teacher plans the pre-emptive feedback in an effort to move students' thinking forwards – and as a way to signal that feedback is an essential feature of the learning process (along with acting on that feedback).

Example 2: Art. The teacher is planning a lesson during which students will be drawing a still life. They have taught such lessons before and therefore have extensive experience on which to call when it comes to identifying pre-emptive feedback. They know the kind of mistakes students are likely to make, as well as the areas on which they could focus to improve what will likely be reasonable first efforts. To this end they develop the following pre-emptive feedback list, and plan to share it with students halfway through the lesson:

- Line. Look at your use of line. Think about how you could better render the lines of the still life. Look at how the still life flows and the kind of shapes you can see within.

- Proportion. Compare the proportions in your drawing with the proportions of the actual still life. Try to tweak your drawing so the proportions are closer to what you can see.

- Perspective. Think about how you have used perspective. Look again at the still life. Consider how your use of perspective has influenced your drawing. Try thinking about how a different perspective might send you down different paths.

- Shading. Look at the way in which you have used shading and whether this achieves what you intended to achieve. Try a different technique on another part of your drawing and compare the impact of the two methods.

- Accuracy. Identify a section of the still life and look intently at this. Consider how accurate your representation is. Look for ways in which you could enhance the accuracy.

- Scale. Compare the different elements of your still life. Ask yourself whether the scale shown in your drawing is the same as the scale you can see. Look for ways in which you could change your drawing so the scale is closer to that of the physical objects.

We see here how the teacher has taken their expertise and used it to create feedback in advance. Students gain access to this midway through the activity and can use it to alter what they are doing. It provokes further thinking, as well as changes in approach.

Another option open to the teacher is to share the pre-emptive feedback before the activity begins. In this formulation, students are encouraged to think about how they might approach the task before they start it, with this thinking informed by the teacher's expertise regarding the likely areas they will overlook or which they might need to work on further down the line.

Distancing

Some students struggle to engage positively with feedback. They may see it as an attack and disengage as a result. This can be due to past experiences, self-perceptions or wider attitudes to learning. One way in which you can overcome the problem, and help students to see feedback in a more positive light, is through distancing. Instead of telling students what you think is good about their work and what could be improved, ask them to work with you to think from someone else's perspective. For example:

- 'If someone else had produced this piece of work, what feedback could we give them?'

- 'If a student at another school brought this work to show us, what could we tell them about it?'

- 'Imagine an expert was looking at this work – a scientist working in a research lab, for example. What might they like about it and what might they suggest to improve it?'

- 'What might a student from the year above think about this work? How might they think it could be improved and what might they like about it?'

- 'If you were the teacher and you were looking at this piece of work, what would you tell me about its strengths? And what might you suggest for an improvement?'

In each of these examples the teacher invites the student into the process of assessment. They do this by asking them to think from someone else's perspective and to use this perspective as a way in which to think critically about their own work. This is how the distance is created. No longer does the student feel feedback is being done to them, instead a level of objectivity is introduced and the feedback takes place at one remove.

This technique does not always work – and it depends to some extent on how defensive the student is about feedback – but it often proves successful. You can also use it as a general tool for helping students to think about their own work, even if they are not particularly likely to disengage from direct feedback. The technique lets students see their work from a different perspective and to think about it through the lens of a third party. This helps them gain revealing insights and is also a way to make them think more critically about what they've produced.

Example 1: Sociology. The teacher hands back a set of essays. They have marked these but, for the moment, are keeping their comments to themselves. Instead, they hand out a sheet explaining what an expert sociologist looks for when they are reading an essay. They then play a video of a sociologist talking about their job, how they write and what they try to achieve with their writing. Next, the teacher invites students to work in pairs to critique their essays, not from their own perspectives but from the perspective of an expert sociologist. Students use the sheet and the ideas from the video as a scaffold.

While this is happening, the teacher circulates and offers further help and support. Once sufficient time has passed, the teacher reveals their own feedback to students – they might do this while they are circulating – and asks them to compare this with what they came up with during their distancing session. The process serves two ends. First, it helps students to look at their work from a different perspective and to critique it in this light. Second, it gives students a chance to compare their distanced assessments with the teacher's point of view. Through the comparison they can reflect critically on their own thinking and build up a better sense of what good looks like.

Example 2: Psychology. The teacher asks students to assess a piece of work they have written and to do this from the perspective of a particular psychological school of thought such as psychodynamics, cognitive psychology or the biological approach. A crib sheet is provided as a support. This outlines the key ideas of the perspective and the kind of things a psychologist of this persuasion would look for.

When students have assessed their own work the teacher challenges them to look at it again, but this time from a different perspective. For example, if students first used the psychodynamic approach to critique their work, now they must use the cognitive approach. Support materials are again handed out and students are encouraged to compare and contrast the results of their two efforts, when they have completed them.

Finally, the teacher provides the class with general feedback connected to the piece of work being examined. Students are then asked to compare this with the results of their own efforts before, finally, coming up with a summary comment they feel offers an accurate representation of the strengths displayed and the one area on which they could focus to improve things.

This process, while a touch convoluted, helps students to develop a broad picture of their work. They assess it through two different perspectives, distancing their thinking in the process, then synthesise their findings with the teacher's own thoughts. Bringing all of this together they are in a position to form a fairly nuanced, fairly detailed judgement about their work and to communicate this with a good amount of evidence on hand to act as a support. Used repeatedly, the technique helps students develop a more critical mindset, meaning they can judge their own work with increasing skill during the process of producing it.

Assessing Famous Work

Another way we can minimise any perceived threat students might attach to receiving feedback is by having them assess famous work. This sees them critiquing work created by experts or leaders in the same field as they are studying. For example, a group of psychology students might critique one of Freud's studies, or a group of English students might assess an extract from Steinbeck.

The purpose is three fold. First, we help students see that critique and the provision of feedback is essentially a neutral process without any moral dimension attached to it. By critiquing famous work we send the message that everything is open to assessment and that, by extension, the work students produce is no exception. Second, we make an implicit connection between the famous work and the work students are creating. While we are not assuming an equivalence, we are indicating that the process of creating work remains the same, even if the content of that process might differ. So, for example, when English students critique an extract from Steinbeck they are critiquing a piece of text produced by the same sort of processes as they are learning about in class.

Third, we take some of the sting out of the process of receiving feedback by helping students to see that anybody – even somebody who is an unalloyed success in their chosen field – can receive critique, and that this is a function of the way in which we apply our minds and understanding to the things we analyse, not a sign that what is being critiqued is eternally lacking or needs its central deficits cast in bright light for all to see. While this might seem melodramatic, these two viewpoints are often implicitly held by many students who find the process of receiving feedback difficult and who get defensive as a result.

Example 1: English. The teacher displays a piece of text on the board and asks students to read through it, discuss it with a partner and then offer a critique. They explain that the text is an extract from a piece of creative writing and indicate that students' critique should focus on identifying two good things and something which could be improved. Finally, the teacher adds that students should try to rewrite part of the text based on the improvement they've identified. This means they are able to both state what should be improved and show how that improvement will look.

After sufficient time has passed, the teacher invites various pairs in the room to share their ideas with the rest of the class. Discussion ensues in which students compare and contrast their critiques. The teacher then reveals that the piece of text students have been assessing is actually an extract from a novel by a famous novelist. For example, George Orwell, Muriel Spark or V.S. Naipaul. At this point, students will likely be a little surprised. And they will be immediately pushed to think again about the critique in which they have just engaged and the wider process of passing judgement. After all, they have unwittingly critiqued a piece of text written by a highly successful, highly praised author.

The teacher concludes the activity by leading students in a discussion about what this might mean. They are careful to draw attention to the equivalence between judging the work of a famous author and students having their own work judged. This helps to make the underlying point of the activity clear for all to see.

Example 2: Photography. The teacher sets up a gallery at one end of the classroom. They use photographs taken by famous photographers, all of which fit with the current theme students are working on. The teacher creates a pro-forma students can use to critique the photographs. This covers various technical and creative aspects.

Students are invited to attend the gallery in small groups – there is not enough space for everyone to go up at once. While they are there, they are expected to examine the photographs and choose one or two to critique using the pro-forma which has been provided. At this point, no information is given regarding the provenance of the pictures.

Once everyone has had a chance to visit the gallery and make their critiques, the teacher rearranges the class into groups. Each group contains students who critiqued different photographs. An exchange now takes place during which learners share their critiques with one another and talk through what they identified as being evidence of good practice and what they thought could have been improved.

When these discussions have run their course, the teacher draws the whole class back together. They display a slide on the board containing some or all of the pictures which constituted the gallery. Each picture is attended by a label indicating who took it. The teacher talks students through the various photographers, signalling their fame, body of work and the high esteem in which they are held.

This is used as a jumping off point for talking about the nature of critique. Students are encouraged to reflect on the assessments they made and to consider whether these would have been different if they had known who had taken the photographs. They are then asked to reflect on their own responses to criticism and feedback, including the extent to which they accept that all photographs are a starting point for discussion and assessment.

Feedback Checklists

You can use feedback checklists to train students to more accurately assess, improve and refine their own work. They are a tool you can teach learners and which, over time, they will likely internalise. This means the checklists become part of learners' minds – something to which they can turn without the need for outside help. For this reason, feedback checklists can be thought of as a metacognitive aid. Something students can use to keep tabs on their own thinking; to improve and cultivate it as they go.

A feedback checklist outlines a series of things students should look for and check in their own work prior to regarding it as a complete. The teacher uses their expert knowledge to construct the checklist, aware in advance of the kind of things students are likely to miss and of the areas to which they need to attend if they want to create the most successful work possible.

For example, a graphic design teacher might develop a feedback checklist based around the different things a student needs to look for in a piece of design work before handing it in to be marked. The purpose here is to transfer the teacher's expertise to a list, which can then be fixed in space and time and shared with the student. Through using the list the student becomes familiar with it. This means they are becoming familiar with the teacher's expertise and, over time, if they remain attentive and engage actively with the list, they start to transfer the expertise into their own mind. Eventually, all being well, they can assess their own work and their own thinking without recourse to the list. This should improve the quality of their work and afford the student a greater degree of control over what they are producing – all as a result of the initial input from the teacher.

Example 1: Graphic Design. The teacher creates the following feedback checklist, which they share with students at the start of the year:

- Ask yourself what would be the first thing someone noticed about your work when they saw it.

- Ask yourself whether your work is a first draft or an improved version.

- Ask yourself what feedback you would give about how your work could be improved – and whether you can make changes before handing it in.

- Ask yourself what you would improve about your work if you only had five minutes. Then see if you can make these changes.

- Ask yourself what I will think when I first see your work – then decide if you want to alter anything.

This feedback checklist provides students with a series of critical positions to cycle through. It promotes a more questioning, critical approach to self-assessment, helping students to think in depth about what they've done, why they've done it and the results to which it's given rise.

Over time, the teacher would expect students to start thinking about the items on the checklist before finishing their work. For example, they might ask themselves whether their work is a first draft or an improved version halfway through, instead of waiting until the end. The aim is to make students better self-assessors by giving them access to the teacher's expertise through the means of the checklist.

Example 2: Citizenship. The teacher creates a feedback checklist which students use every time they produce a longer piece of written work:

- Read through your work before handing it in. Does it make sense? Does it say what you want it to say? Don't be afraid to make changes if it doesn't.

- Check your language. How much is slang? Have you used enough technical vocabulary? Are there any important keywords you've forgotten to include?

- Think about your audience. Who were you writing for? Does what you have written fit for the intended audience – or do you need to make some tweaks?

- Examine your analysis. Have you gone into detail? Have you explained everything? You might need to include some more examples or make some extra points. Add these in if you think they're necessary.

- Look at your evaluation. Where could you have been more critical? How else could you have evaluated the different ideas and arguments? Are there things you can add now, before handing in your work?

This checklist helps students see their work through the eyes of the teacher. It is like feedback before the event, helping and encouraging the student to critically reflect on what they've produced before handing it over for marking. There is an expectation that as part of this reflection students will make changes and improve their work.

Chapter Eight – Further Marking Techniques

Introduction

In this chapter we examine a selection of marking techniques not mentioned elsewhere. The purpose is to provide further strategies on which you can draw to maximise the effectiveness and efficiency of your marking. Each technique is explained and then exemplified through two different areas of the curriculum. This helps to provide context and demonstrate how you might choose to apply the technique. The chapter builds on points made earlier in the book – especially those contained in Chapters Two and Three. These won't be repeated here, but they are implicit in what follows.

Category List

When we judge a piece of work we do so through a set of expert lenses. These lenses are comprised of the different categories we associate with the subject in question. For example, an art teacher might look at categories such as originality and use of line whereas a PE teacher might look at ones like technique and commitment. When assessing student work – when making judgements – we invoke these categories, often without an awareness of what we are doing. We then use them to help us make a comparison.

Does this painting show a good degree of originality? Well, compared to my existing understanding of the category – my expert understanding – I would say no, it doesn't. Therefore I can give useful feedback on this area.

Did the student demonstrate good technique when throwing the javelin? Compared to my expert understanding I would say the technique was good as she approached the line but less good as she threw, so I can give feedback on the latter.

If we accept that we use categories to make judgements about student work then we can speed up the marking process by sitting down and making a list of these categories. We can then keep this list to hand while we mark and refer to it when we come to write our feedback. This quickens the process and means we always have a set of areas on hand to which we can look when deciding what feedback would be most useful.

Example 1: History. At the start of the year the history teacher sits down and makes two lists: a general category list covering the key areas they look for when marking the work of any student and a set of lists covering additional categories they might look for depending on the age of the student. They keep these lists somewhere close to hand and take them out whenever they come to mark student work. They place the relevant lists on their desk and refer to them as they do their marking. Specifically, they use the lists as a basis for the targets they set. First they read what students have written, then they identify a series of strengths, then they select a category the student needs to work on and use this to construct an appropriate target.

Example 2: English. The English teacher makes a list of the key categories they use to make judgements about creative writing at A Level. They share this list with their students, explaining that it is through these lenses that they will be making judgements. This has the benefit of helping students to understand where the teacher is coming from, what good looks like, and what areas of understanding they need to develop if they are to become better creative writers. Through the course of the year the teacher marks student work, focussing on one or two categories at a time. They tie both their positive and developmental feedback to these, meaning students are consistently encouraged to reflect on, think about and respond to information predicated on key categories inherent to successful creative writing.

Strengths Chart

Here's another technique you can use to speed up your marking. Instead of spending time thinking about the strengths demonstrated by a piece of student work, create a chart containing a wide range of strengths appropriate to the subject or subjects you teach. You can then refer to this while you are marking. Simply look at the chart and either identify a relevant strength you can include in your feedback verbatim, or take one of the existing strengths included in your chart and rewrite it so it fits with the work in front of you.

There are a couple of ways in which you can construct your strengths chart. First, you can sit down at the start of the year and make a list of categories you use to make judgements (here there is overlap with the previous technique). Having done this, you can come up with five to ten key strengths for each category, capturing all the information in a spreadsheet or MS Word document.

Second, you can collate the strengths you convey to students through your written feedback as you go. This method is more cumbersome but does have the virtue of producing a chart containing strengths written exactly as you would want to write them in student books.

Whichever option you select, the result is the same. You end up with an extensive collection of ready-made strengths you can apply to the work you mark. This doesn't mean you are ignoring the work students produce and picking strengths off the shelf to make your life easy. Far from it. Instead, you are doing some of the analytical work in advance by coming up with and storing relevant strengths. Your marking then focusses on identifying which of the already collated strengths are appropriate to the piece of work you are looking at, meaning you don't have to divide your mind between assessing what is in front of you and manufacturing appropriate strengths off the cuff.

Example 1: PE. At the start of the year the PE teacher sits down and makes a list of ten categories they will use to assess the theory side of their students' GCSE work. Having done this, they go through each category and identify five key strengths they will be looking for as the year progresses. They also leave space to add additional strengths to each category, combining both methods outlined above. As the term progresses and they start marking student work, they use their strengths chart as a reference point. On some occasions they find they can copy strengths they have identified directly into their written feedback. On other occasions they have to make a few tweaks and adjustments. All this saves them time and helps them to mark both efficiently and effectively.

Example 2: Art. As the year progresses, the art teacher makes a point of recording the different strengths they share with students through their written feedback. They sort these strengths into relevant categories and, gradually, develop a strengths chart which, by the end of the year, is full of different strengths covering a wide range of categories connected to their teaching. The following year, they are able to draw a twin benefit. First, they can use the strengths chart to significantly speed up their marking – in much the same way as the PE example. Second, they can share some or all of the strengths chart with their students, helping them to better understand what good looks like and what they need to be focussing on to improve their work.

Highlighting

When we highlight student work the eye is immediately drawn to the different colours on the page. This can help students to better understand what feedback you are giving or to what section of their work your feedback refers. Another advantage is that highlighting can be done quickly and with minimum effort; it adds little to your marking workload and may even subtract from it. Let us consider two key ways in which you can use highlighting.

First, you can highlight different parts of a student's work, then write your feedback at the end, alongside a key indicating the relationship between the highlighting colours and what you have written. For example, we might have three highlighters – red, blue and green. We go through a student's essay and highlight some parts in red, some in blue and some in green. At the end we write a detailed comment outlining two key strengths and suggesting one area for improvement. We also create a key similar to the following:

First strength = Red highlighting

Second strength = Blue highlighting

Area for Improvement = Green highlighting

This method means it is really easy for students to see how your feedback connects to the piece of work they have produced. It also makes it easier for them to refer back to your comments in the future. For example, in two lessons' time we might ask the imaginary student to remind themselves of their area for improvement. They can flick back through their book, find the relevant page and immediately see the green highlighting reminding them what they need to work on.

Second, you can highlight a section of a student's work and then write your feedback exclusively about this. The benefit here is that the highlighting causes the student to zone in on the area of their work you most want them to think about. For example, we might have a Year 6 learner who has written up a report of a science experiment. Much of this is good but we also notice one area in which they have not understood what was expected of them. As such, we decide the best option is to focus our feedback on this, so they know what to do differently next time. We highlight the relevant section and write our feedback at the end of the report. When the work is returned to the student they can quickly find the area to which our feedback refers and can then analyse it in light of our comments.

Example 1: Maths. A maths teacher marks using a pen and two highlighters. They use the pen to tick correct answers and to write any formative comments at the end of the student's work. They use the first highlighter to indicate careless mistakes. That is, incorrect answers which the student could have avoided if they had checked their work more carefully or paid more attention as they were doing it. The second highlighter is used to indicate useful mistakes, that is, mistakes based on misconceptions or faulty technique. These are mistakes from which the student can learn. Students are trained to understand the method favoured by the teacher and are thus in a position to act on the marking when their work is returned to them.

Example 2: Sociology. A sociology teacher explains to their class that they want to see a greater use of contemporary examples and that these should be relevant, original and well-explained. When marking student work they use three highlighter pens. The first colour is used to denote areas where a contemporary example could have been used but wasn't.

The second colour is used to indicate contemporary examples which are not as relevant or original as they could be. And the third colour is used to highlight contemporary examples which meet the criteria set out at the start. All of this results in students getting work returned to them which is easy to analyse and from which they can quickly and effectively come up with their own targets.

Marking Codes

You can use a set of marking codes to communicate information swiftly and precisely to students. Instead of writing a series of comments around their work, or underlining and circling a range of different areas, you can simply note down the codes wherever they are most appropriate. When you return work to students, you can invite them to look through the codes and make any changes deemed necessary – or simply use the information to improve their next attempt.

When coming up with a set of marking codes, avoid developing too many. Focus instead on creating a handful which cover the most useful and relevant areas of your marking. These will be areas that crop up again and again. That you are regularly asking students to look at, correct and improve. For example, an English teacher might come up with the following code:

Sp = Spelling – check the spelling of one or more words in this line.

P = Punctuation – check the punctuation in this line.

S = Sense – reread this sentence to see if it makes sense.

NP = New Paragraph – you need to start a new paragraph here.

IU = Incorrect Usage – check your usage of words in this line.

We have five codes here, covering most of the key areas the teacher will look at when marking student work. The codes don't cover everything, but they cover enough to be useful – both to students and the teacher. When marking work, the teacher can speed up the process. They can use the codes to quickly communicate accurate information to students. In turn, students can act on this information when they get their books back, because they are familiar with the codes. Thought of in this way, we can see that marking codes are essentially a version of shorthand shared between teacher and student.

To help students remember the meaning of the codes, provide a small handout for them to stick in the front of their books. After a few pieces of work have been marked, most students will internalise the codes and know what they mean.

Another advantage of using marking codes is that, over time, you can train students to self-assess their work in line with the codes. For example, our English teacher might ask their students to read through their work looking at Sp, P, S, NP and IU before they hand it in. They might even go a step further and specify that they want to see at least two corrections made by every student before the work is deemed ready to be marked.

Example 1: Literacy. The Year 5 teacher who teaches literacy comes up with a code similar to the one above. They use this to help students develop a better understanding of where they are making mistakes. After marking student work, the teacher hands it back, displays the codes on the board as a reminder, and invites students to go through and examine what they have written. Students are challenged to correct at least half of the mistakes the teacher has identified. This process sees learners taking ownership of their work and responding to the marking codes so as to bring about improvements.

Example 2: Geography. The geography teacher creates the following code:

T = Technical language – check your usage in this sentence.

E = Examples – look at your use of examples, how could this have been different?

Exp = Explanation – check your explanation; is it accurate and could you have said more?

Ev = Evaluation – how else could you have evaluated here?

They use this code to mark student work, teaming it up with a general formative comment at the end focussing on strengths and a target. When students get their work back, the first ten minutes are taken up with them reading through the marking codes and making changes, additions and excisions based on what the teacher has indicated. From time to time, the teacher sets students the challenge of focussing on one of the four areas (T, E, Exp or Ev) while producing their work. This helps them to focus their attention on some of the key aspects of creating good quality work in geography.

Verbal Marking

Developments in information technology mean you can now capture verbal marking of written work. For example, some pieces of software let students submit their work electronically. You can then read through this work and record yourself marking it. This verbal narration gives students a completely different way to access your expertise and assimilate formative feedback. A teacher receiving a student's essay might record themselves talking about each aspect of it in turn, drawing attention as they go to specific areas which are good and those areas which need to be improved.

Verbal marking of this type can be particularly useful for a number of reasons. First, students can listen to your voice at the same time as they look at their work. This dual sensory input can help them to make swifter connections than might otherwise be the case between your analysis and what they have done. Second, students can pause, rewind and replay your feedback, accessing it in a different way to written information. Third, recording verbal feedback fixes it in time and space – turning it into verbal marking. This removes the ephemeral aspect of speech and means students can return to it as they wish – something which isn't possible with the unrecorded spoken word.

One of the risks of using verbal marking is that you may find yourself being verbose. Written comments have a discipline attached to them. We might restrict ourselves to three strengths and a target, or we might decide that we will write only a single paragraph for each student. Either way, we have set a limit on the amount of information we are prepared to convey. Verbal marking has the potential to go way past this. You start recording yourself talking about the work a student has produced and, before you know it, you've been rambling on for five minutes.

Now, that may not sound like a long time but, trust me, it is. To illustrate, go and watch a YouTube video of that length and compare what it would feel like for a student to have to listen to an unstructured analysis of their work lasting the same length of time.

To avoid this problem, a couple of rules are worth following. First, set yourself a time limit and stick to it. What this is will depend on the age group with whom you are working and, to some extent, the complexity of the work students have created. However, I would always say that less is more and you may well find that 30 – 45 seconds is plenty of time to convey useful, tailored information. Second, structure your narration just as you would structure a piece of written feedback. For example, stick to three strengths and a target. Or, pick three elements of the student's work and talk about each of these in turn, signalling that you are doing this as you go. This should help you create condensed, rich recordings of verbal feedback through which students can access your expertise and understand how to improve their work.

Example 1: Chemistry. The chemistry teacher sets students the task of balancing a range of equations and submitting their work electronically. They then look through this online, recording their feedback for each student. They decide to focus on the mistakes students have made. For each one, they offer a quick explanation of where the student has gone wrong and why this has happened. They support their explanation, and develop student understanding, by contrasting the mistakes with the equations students have correctly balanced. This helps students to better understand where they have gone wrong and why they have been successful at other times.

Example 2: Philosophy. The philosophy teacher sets students an essay, collects these electronically and then records themselves giving verbal feedback. They decide to give three strengths and a target, using this as a way to structure their feedback and ensure they don't start to ramble. When narrating their marking of the essays they use a highlighter function in MS Word to indicate the areas of the work to which they are referring. When students receive their feedback they can both hear what the teacher is saying and immediately see the area to which they are referring. The teacher challenges students to implement their targets in the next essay – and to record a 30-second narration explaining how successful they have been in attempting this.

Tell Me What to Mark

Usually, it falls to us to decide what to mark. And, invariably, we decide to mark most things, if not all. While we might not give equal weight to all elements, prioritising some over others, for example, we tend to at least make sure we've covered all the work a student has done. Selection, though, is often a good thing. We might decide to only mark certain pieces of work a student has produced – those pieces which give us the most useful access to their current knowledge, understanding and ability. Or, we might turn it over to our students and ask them to tell us what we should mark.

The aim of this approach is to place the onus on the student. They have to analyse their own work and make a reasoned judgement about where teacher feedback will be most useful. We encourage them to look critically at what they've done, and to discriminate between different aspects of it.

For example, learners might be writing poems over the course of three English lessons. Let us imagine that, on average, each learner creates five poems by the end of the third lesson. The teacher doesn't want to mark all five poems every learner has created. In part, because this would not be an efficacious use of their time. So, they say the following: 'In the next five minutes, I want you to look through the poems you've written. Select one that you want me to mark. This might be your best, or the one you feel it would be most useful to have feedback on. When you've selected your poem, write me a brief paragraph explaining why you choose it and why you think it will be worth my while marking it and giving you feedback.'

With these words the dynamic of the classroom changes. Students are now in control. They have to look discriminatingly at what they have produced, make a judgement and then justify this to the teacher. In turn, the teacher finds themselves in a different position. They no longer have to look through student work and mark everything – or decide what to mark. Instead, this has been done for them. They can focus all their attention on giving useful, relevant feedback on the poems students have identified. If they feel something is wrong with a student's choice they are still in a position to refer back to their other poems as well.

Example 1: Art. After a number of weeks students have filled up twenty or so pages of their sketchbooks. The art teacher wants to take these in so they can mark them and give some feedback. They set aside the last ten minutes of the lesson. Students use this time to look through their sketchbooks and select three pages on which they would like feedback. They mark these pages with a small cross in the top right-hand corner. The teacher takes the sketchbooks in and can quickly find the pages each student wants them to look at.

Example 2: Dance. Students are putting together a video portfolio of self-choreographed routines. These are stored on the school's intranet. After a few weeks, most students have amassed several videos – some recorded in lessons, some outside lessons. The teacher sets students the following homework task: 'Look through your portfolios and select one video you want me to watch and on which you would like me to provide detailed feedback.' Students bring their decisions to the next lesson and the teacher makes a note of these. They subsequently watch the videos requested by the students and give detailed feedback focussing on what is good and how the routines could be improved.

Target Implementation Marking

We set students targets with the expectation that they will try to implement these. If they do, so our thinking goes, then their work will improve and they will make good progress. If they don't, then they will probably keep doing what they were already doing – and there will be less progress as a result.

Target implementation marking is where we assess the extent to which students have successfully implemented the targets we set them. Our aim is to work out whether students have been able to change their work, based on our feedback. We are also interested in whether or not students have had difficulty in implementing the targets we set. If they have, we can offer further support. On the other hand, if it appears that targets have been too easily implemented then we can think about setting more difficult ones in future.

Timing is key when using target implementation marking. You must ensure that students have recently completed a piece of work in which they attempted to put their targets into practice. Otherwise, you are going to be marking work which may not have much of a connection to students' present targets. A good option is to follow a structure like this:

- Set a piece of work.

- Take in student work and mark it. Provide formative feedback, including a target.

- Return the work to students.

- Plan an activity or task in which students have an opportunity to implement their targets.

- Ask students to write their targets at the top of the page before they begin.

- Take in student work.

- Mark the work, focussing on the extent to which students have successfully implemented their targets.

Note the fifth bullet point. This serves a dual purpose. First, it helps keep students on track. If their target is visible then chances are they will have it at the forefront of their minds as they work. Second, it makes your marking easier. You don't need to look back through student books to find the last target you gave them. They have written it out for you as a reminder. You can easily compare their work with their target and assess the extent to which they have successfully implemented it.

When giving feedback on target implementation, you can use the traditional three strengths and an area for improvement model. Or, you can approach it as a zero-sum game: the student has either implemented their target or they haven't. If they have, you can set them a new one. If they haven't, you can give them feedback explaining what has happened and what they need to change next time. A third and final option is to adopt the highlighting method and to use this to signal where the student has successfully implemented their target and where they have fallen short. The student can then quickly see which bits of their work they need to improve and which bits demonstrate success.

Example 1: Psychology. The teacher marks student work and sets everyone in the class a target. Students are asked to focus on this during the next couple of lessons. At the start of each lesson they write their target at the top of the page and then try to implement it. The teacher plans activities and tasks which give students ample opportunity to do this.

When the teacher collects in student books they mark them and give feedback focussed on whether or not students have successfully implemented their targets. When books are returned, the teacher leads the class in a ten minute respond, review and reflect activity. They use part of this time as a chance to talk to the group as a whole about target implementation techniques and some of the patterns and trends they observed while marking the books.

Example 2: Literacy. The Year 6 teacher sets learners a persuasive writing task. They take in the work learners produce, mark this and provide feedback. Every learner ends up with a specific target they need to work on to improve the quality of their persuasive writing. Learners get their work back and the teacher spends some time ensuring that everybody understands their target – both what it means and how to implement it. At the start of the following week the teacher sets a new persuasive writing task. They explain that during this learners should focus on trying to implement their targets. The teacher collects in the work learners produce and marks this. They focus on assessing the extent to which targets have been successfully implemented and give feedback on this.

If a learner has been successful, the teacher praises them, justifying that praise through reference to specific things the learner has done, and then sets a new target. If a learner has not been successful, the teacher explains where they have fallen short and offers advice on how they can rectify this next time around. Finally, learners get their work back, along with their feedback, and the teacher leads the class in a reflection activity during which everybody has a chance to think about their feedback, get support from the teacher and decide how they will try to change their work in the future.

Chapter Nine – Exemplar Questions

You can use questions as a type of feedback, although they do not work in the same way as traditional feedback. The sentence types make different demands on the individuals who receive them. To demonstrate, consider these two examples:

A) You need to develop your points in more detail. Try to include at least one example each time.

B) How could you develop your points in more detail? Could examples be an option?

A is an example of traditional feedback. B is an example of feedback in the form of questions. In A, the sentences direct the receiver to act in certain ways; they are almost like commands. In B, the sentences invoke the typical rules of questioning; they invite the receiver to respond.

The difference is subtle. Using questions means you are asking students to do a little more of the work. This can be challenging; it can also be rewarding. In the example above, A provides students with a clear understanding of what needs to be done. B implies something similar, but a degree of ambiguity remains. The student is asked to think for themselves and to make a decision, while prompted to think about a specific subject (level of detail) defined by the teacher.

There is no definitive method for judging when questions are appropriate. Some teachers regularly deliver feedback in the form of questions. Others do so rarely. And a good number use a mixture of question-based and traditional feedback.

The purpose of this chapter is to provide a collection of exemplar questions you can use to deliver feedback, or modify to suit your needs. This will help you to decide whether question-based feedback is right for you and the students with whom you work. It also gives you a starting point for engaging in some trial and error – and seeing how different students respond.

I have chosen ten categories through which to divide up the questions. These categories are repeated in the next chapter, which covers feedback of the traditional kind. The categories are not exhaustive, but they do cover a wide range of areas applicable across the curriculum.

Mistakes

1. How can you tell this is a mistake?

2. Which of the mistakes can we learn the most from?

3. Why do you think you made these mistakes?

4. How could you avoid making the same mistakes in the future?

5. What does this mistake tell you about what you need to do next?

6. Why is this part of your work the bit which caused you to go wrong?

7. Which of the mistakes are easiest to fix?

8. How can you avoid similar mistakes next time?

9. What changes could you make so you pick up on mistakes before you hand your work in?

10. How could this bit of your work [the mistake] look different? What would you need to do to change it?

11. I've identified three mistakes. Can you find them and tell me why they are mistakes?

12. How could you use your mistakes to improve your next piece of work?

13. Can you come up with a way to avoid making these same mistakes again?

14. What might explain why you made these mistakes? How could you rectify them?

15. Where have you made the most mistakes? Why do you think this is – and what do we need to do next?

Process

1. How could changing your planning improve your work?

2. Would checking have made a difference? Why?

3. What steps did you go through? Did you miss any out?

4. Could you have spent more time on designing? What difference might it have made?

5. When did you get distracted? Can you tell from looking at your work?

6. How did you decide on this approach? What other approaches could you have considered?

7. What was the most important decision you made? How did you make it?

8. What order did you do things in? Was that the best order? Why?

9. How did you apply the formula? How does this compare to my method?

10. What do you think you missed? If you'd done things differently, would you have missed it?

11. Where do you think the problem started? Was it in the planning?

12. Why didn't you achieve what you wanted? Did you have too many things to think about?

13. If you were going to do it again, what would you do differently?

14. How important was taking careful notes during the experiment? Why?

15. Could you have taken longer on this bit? What difference might it have made?

Content

1. What's missing here? Go back over your notes and tell me.

2. What stopped you using more keywords?

3. How could you check the information is right before handing in?

4. Which of the studies did you spend least time on? Why?

5. Why did you choose to focus on only one area of the play?

6. What questions did you ask yourself when you read the source? What questions could you have asked yourself?

7. How could this be more detailed? What three changes could you make?

8. Have a look at the bits I've circled. Why might these need looking at a second time?

9. How might an expert tweak this so that it was more precise?

10. Which of your answers is most accurate? Why are the others less accurate?

11. Did you follow the recipe? How can you tell?

12. Does this explain or describe the idea? Can you remind me of the difference?

13. Why are these examples of incorrect usage? How could you ensure you use them correctly in the future?

14. Of the three examples, which is the weakest? Why?

15. What makes your second answer better than your first?

Understanding

1. Which bit did you understand the least? Can you see evidence of this in your work?

2. How could you try to improve your understanding of X?

3. What do you need to do next to understand X better?

4. Where did your understanding let you down? What could you do to change things?

5. Did you understand the task before you started? What could you do next time?

6. How could you show me more of what you understand?

7. In what ways could you change this so I can better see what you understand?

8. Where did your understanding of the formula start to run up against problems? Why do you think this was?

9. How did your understanding change as you were writing the essay?

10. Could you have used some planning time to further develop your understanding? What impact might this have had?

11. What does good understanding look like?

12. When you used the keywords, did you understand all of them?

13. Which question was hardest to understand? What can you do to change this?

14. Can you show me which bits you understood the most and which you understood the least?

15. Is your understanding the same now as when you started the work? Why?

Targets

1. Where did you best meet your target? Where could you improve things?

2. How has your work changed due to focussing on your target?

3. What else could you have done to meet your target?

4. How will you continue to meet your target?

5. What improvements can you see in your work? Why are they improvements?

6. How did your target change your approach?

7. What differences did your target give rise to?

8. Where is the evidence that you implemented your target? Why is it evidence?

9. What makes your work different now that you have met your target?

10. Where were you thinking most about your target? Where least?

11. What can you learn from trying to implement your target?

12. What do you think your next target should be and why?

13. How could you challenge yourself with a new target?

14. Can you suggest a target to aim for next?

15. Was your target too easy? Why? How could it have been more challenging?

Knowledge

1. Where did you struggle most for knowledge? What could you do to improve things?

2. Were there certain things you didn't know? How could you find out about them?

3. What made it difficult to apply your knowledge? How could you work on this?

4. What do you know now that you didn't before? What do you need to know next?

5. Why was it difficult to use your knowledge here?

6. What gaps in your knowledge can you identify?

7. How would you rate your knowledge for each of the different sections?

8. Could you have included more detail here? What difference would that have made?

9. Why did you include lots of detail at the start but not at the end?

10. What could you do to ensure you have more examples to use in the future?

11. How could you improve your vocabulary so you have more technical words to use?

12. If this explanation is wrong, how could you find out the right one?

13. If this isn't the best theory for explaining it, where else could you look?

14. If this analysis isn't sufficiently in-depth, what else will you need to learn about?

15. If this comparison doesn't work, what further research might you need to do?

Editing/Rewriting

1. Which section do you think needs the most rewriting?

2. How could editing have improved this?

3. Can you choose one question to rewrite? Why that question and how will you improve it?

4. Why might this sentence be better if you wrote it differently?

5. If you had to edit your plan, what changes would you make to the first section?

6. Can you tell me how you could rewrite the conclusion so it is punchier?

7. How might more editing in the design phase have resulted in a better product?

8. Which equations should we rewrite? Why?

9. If you had to start again from scratch, what changes would you make and why?

10. How could you use what you learned from editing to improve your future work?

11. Can you rewrite the character's speech so it sounds more realistic?

12. Why might editing have prevented these mistakes?

13. How could you use editing to stop these problems recurring in the future?

14. Can you rewrite your answers to questions 3, 7 and 11, but this time focus on applying your target?

15. Can you tell me three ways that editing would improve this piece of work?

Effort

1. Where did you put in the most effort? Why?

2. Where did you put in the least effort? What impact did this have?

3. How could you sustain your effort for longer next time?

4. How would you judge your level of effort? What could you do to raise this?

5. Did you focus your effort all the way through? Why?

6. Can you show me the areas where you put in the most effort? What made you do this?

7. Why did your effort drop off at the end? What can you learn from this?

8. Could you have managed your effort levels differently?

9. What made it difficult for you to maintain your effort?

10. How would this work be different if you'd put in more effort?

11. When did your effort levels start to dip? What could you do differently next time?

12. Why did your effort levels go up and down during the task? What can you learn from this?

13. Where was it most enjoyable to put in a high level of effort? Why?

14. Can you explain what it felt like to keep trying when it got tough? How can you make sure you do this again in the future?

15. If you had to judge your effort on a scale of 1-10, what would you go for and why? How could you get a 10 next time?

Challenge

1. How could you challenge yourself next time?

2. What would a challenging target look like based on this piece of work?

3. What part was most challenging and why? What can you learn from this?

4. How did you keep yourself going when the challenge increased? What could you do next time?

5. How much were you in control of the level of challenge? What evidence is there for this?

6. What impact did the level of challenge have on your work?

7. Can you show me where the level of challenge was too high? What can we learn from this?

8. What strategies did you use to deal with challenges? Can you use these again in the future?

9. Where was it hardest to implement your target? What made this a challenge?

10. When did you feel the level of challenge getting too much? What does this tell us?

11. Why did you settle for the easier challenge? How could you push yourself in the future?

12. How did you approach the challenge? Would a different approach have been better?

13. If you had to set yourself a more challenging task, what would it be and why?

14. Can you explain what the right level of challenge is for you at the moment?

15. What does it feel like when you are being really challenged? Could you use this to help yourself in the future?

Strengths

1. Can you show me three things you've done well?

2. What strengths are there in your work?

3. Where were you successful – and how do you know you were?

4. How did you make progress in this piece of work?

5. Why is this a good piece of work?

6. What did you do well today – and what evidence do you have to prove it?

7. Where did you show your strengths?

8. How is your work better now than it was three weeks ago?

9. Where did you make the biggest improvements today?

10. How has your target helped you to get better?

11. Why did this piece of work play to your strengths?

12. How did you use your strengths to create a good piece of work?

13. When did your strengths come into play – and why?

14. If you could identify a key strength of your work, what would it be and why?

15. If you had to pick out the most pleasing part of your work, what would you choose?

Chapter Ten – Exemplar Targets

In this chapter you will find 150 examples of effective targets. These complement the question-based feedback exemplars from the last chapter. They also provide a basis for trying things out with your own students. You can use the examples as they are written, or adapt them to suit your needs and the needs of your learners. The categorisation is the same as the previous chapter and, as there, is wide-ranging but not exhaustive.

In each case, the emphasis is on giving students clear information they can use to channel their future efforts. Often, targets would be delivered at the same time as strengths. Here, however, I have decided to focus only on the former as these are easier to exemplify without direct recourse to student work. None of the targets are set in stone. Feel free to modify as you see fit. But they do give a sense of what good looks like and can also be used as a launch-pad for your own thinking.

Finally, you can find my free resource 'The Feedback Compendium' on my website – www.mikegershon.com/resources/. This contains a large selection of exemplar feedback which you might also like to use, adapt or take as a starting point for your own efforts.

Mistakes

1. Focus on avoiding the mistakes I've identified. Notice how these tend to come as you're nearing the end of a section. Remind yourself to stay focussed at this point in your work.

2. Check the meaning of any keywords you're uncertain about, then include them in your writing. This will help you to avoid misusing words in the future.

3. Take a look at the mistake I've identified and the corrected example I've written next to it. Refer to this while you are writing your next story to avoid it happening again.

4. Try to use the checklist I've provided every time you sit down to start a practical. This will help you avoid making the same mistake again.

5. Next time, ensure you check your calculations forwards and backwards. This will help you to identify and then rectify a higher number of mistakes.

6. Notice how you mistook the denominator for the numerator in a number of the later calculations. Check this carefully before you start each sum – label them if you need to.

7. Your work shows more mistakes when you're rushing to finish. I don't mind if you don't get everything done in the time – I'd like you to focus on not making mistakes instead.

8. Have a look at my example. Note how I first describe and then explain. I'd like you to practice doing this each time you answer a question. Try to avoid just describing.

9. When you receive the ball you're taking your eye off it. That's why you're making mistakes with your control. Focus on keeping your eye on the ball until it gets to you.

10. Your stitching has a lot of mistakes in the more complex sections. Go back and practice the different stitches we've learned in the last couple of lessons, then try again.

11. Make a note of the mistakes I've highlighted. Next time, keep this list to hand and use it to stop yourself making the same mistakes again.

12. Some of your sentences don't make sense. I'd like you to read your work out to yourself before you hand it in. Then you can spot the mistakes and change them before I read it.

13. Watch me cutting the wood. Notice how I keep the cutting motion smooth. Can you see the difference between that and what you were doing? Next time, just concentrate on keeping that smooth motion.

14. You added an extra paragraph in here which actually takes away from the argument instead of adding to it. Next time, ask yourself if you need to add anything extra, or whether what you've done is stronger when left as it is.

15. A good rule of thumb is to work through the sums backwards, checking each one. That way you're more likely to spot mistakes. Try to apply it next time.

Process

1. A really good approach is to break your plan down into three sections and only move on when you've completed each one. I'd like to see you trying that out in your next piece of work.

2. Think about what you want the reader to get from your story before you start writing. You can then use this to make decisions about what to write.

3. If you find yourself getting stuck again, don't give up. First try using a different strategy to solve the problem, then try asking a friend or looking in a book. If you still can't do it, come and ask me.

4. Positively visualise what you want to do before you do it. This will help you get closer to producing an error-free routine. Try it out the next time you practice.

5. Record your data twice, using the system I've shown you. This will make it easier for you to check the accuracy of your measurements.

6. Think about the order of your paragraphs after you've planned what you want to write. Compare how different orders might have different results.

7. Try to use more descriptive language in your writing. A good technique is to identify some key words and phrases in advance. You can then work these in as you go.

8. Make a note of the difference between analysis and critique. You might like to include some examples as well. The next time we do a mock exam, use this to help you decide how to answer these types of questions.

9. Try asking yourself these questions the next time we do some design work: What do I want to achieve? How do I want the end product to look? What might get in my way?

10. Next time I'd like you to try making a different choice. See what happens and then tell me what differences you notice.

11. A useful technique is to read each page in full, then to make a short summary or series of bullet points. Try it out and see how you get on.

12. When analysing a question, don't forget that you can reframe the question so it's easier for you to play to your strengths.

13. Try looking for difficult words first, sounding them out and then reading the sentence in full.

14. I'd like to see more originality in your work. Think of the famous pieces we've been studying as a starting point for your own ideas, not as something you need to copy.

15. If you get to the end and get a result which seems wrong, go back and check each stage of your calculations in turn. Dividing it up makes it easier to isolate an error.

Content

1. When using keywords make sure you are using them carefully. I'd like to see you checking your keyword usage before you hand your work in.

2. I'm pleased you've tried to use the new ideas we've been learning about. Compare how you've used them with the example I've written out. I'd like you to try using them in this way next time round.

3. Use examples to explain some of the new ideas we learned about. This will help you to better understand them and will also show me that you understand them.

4. Your explanation is less detailed than it could be. Try breaking the information down into separate sections and explaining each part in turn.

5. I can see from your work that you've really remembered the first part of the lesson. Try going back and reminding yourself of what we did in the second half. I'd like to see a similar level of detail for that material.

6. A good way to analyse a source is to compare it to your existing knowledge. That way you can identify which bits are most believable and which bits might require some extra thinking or research.

7. Increase the level of detail in your work by doing more reading before you start writing. This will ensure you have more information and ideas you can bring in.

8. I've seen you using the same ideas on a few occasions now. These are good and I like how you use them, but in your next piece of work I'd like you to bring in some of the new material we're learning about.

9. You don't need to include everything in every answer. Read the question carefully and select the pieces of information you think are most important. We can discuss your choices after the next set of questions.

10. Try to include a greater variety of keywords in your work. This shows wider content knowledge and means you can bring in more information.

11. This keyword has an important technical meaning. It's different from how you've used it here. Remind yourself of the meaning and see if you can use the keyword more effectively next time.

12. For each major idea we've looked at in the last three weeks, see if you can come up with two really strong examples. Make a note of these and then be ready to use them in future.

13. I'd like you to try explaining the key idea in a different way. A good starting point is to show how it connects to what you already know about the topic. Try going from there.

14. Practice writing in more detail by including two key pieces of information in each of your paragraphs. You might like to identify what these will be before you start.

15. You haven't quite described the ideas as accurately as you could have done. Take a look at your explanation of electromagnetism. This could include more technical language and less common language.

Understanding

1. Demonstrate your understanding by showing me what you know. In some of your project there is too much copy and paste. Developing good understanding means putting ideas into your own words.

2. Illustrate your understanding by using examples which link to the topic. This will make your work more relevant and will show me that your understanding is at a deeper level.

3. In the third question you could have pushed yourself further by going into more detail and showing that you fully understand the ideas. I'd like you to apply this approach in your next piece of work.

4. The conclusion to your write-up makes the findings sound black and white. I think there is more to them than that. Go back, take another look and see if you can show me where the shades of grey are.

5. Explain your answers in full – including working out. If I can't see this then I can't be sure that you fully understand. Take what's in your head and show it to me on the page.

6. There's a couple of points here where you've gone off task. You can only show your full understanding if you keep focussed on the task all the way through. Next time, keep reminding yourself of this to stay on track.

7. Show me what you can do! This project is good but not as in-depth as I know you can make it. Pick one section and put everything into it – show me what you really know!

8. I'd like you to challenge your understanding of the Crimean War by researching interpretations which don't agree with what you think. See if you can use these to develop your own ideas.

9. Instead of saying half a dozen of one and six of the other I'd like you to give me a definite conclusion. What do you think? Show me you understand the topic by settling on a more meaningful judgement.

10. I think this leaflet shows there are some gaps in your understanding. Have a look at the places I've marked and come up with a list of things we should look at again.

11. Compare your routine to the video I've made. See if you can identify where our understanding of the brief differs. I'd like you to use what you find to develop your routine.

12. Convince me that you really understand calculus. It's up to you what you use, but I want you to focus on communicating to me what it's for, how it works and why it matters.

13. I think there are two or three things you could have included to better show your understanding. Have a look at the list I've made and decide which you want to work on next time.

14. Before you start on your next piece of work, I'd like you to think about how well you understand each idea. If you identify one that you don't really understand, take some time to talk to me about it before you begin.

15. Bring in a wider range of ideas and information to show me that you fully understand what we've been discussing. If you're not sure, focus on a smaller number at first and then ask me for help.

Targets

1. Take a look at your last target. I think you're getting close to achieving this, but there's still a little way to go. I'd like you to review your target while you're completing your next piece of work. Keep reminding yourself of it to stay on track.

2. You've definitely managed to implement your target here. I want you to keep going with it for the moment – prove to me you've really got the hang of it.

3. You haven't quite put your target into practice in this piece of work. I'd like you to try again with it. Have a look at the areas I've circled and see if you can avoid making the same mistakes next time.

4. You've met your target really well in the first set of questions. In the second, you've lost a bit of focus. I'd like you to concentrate on analysing your own performance next time, before you hand your work in. Use your target as a lens to look through.

5. I think you should set your own target now. You've successfully achieved what I asked you to do. Now you need to decide what the next improvement is that you can work on.

6. That target obviously wasn't challenging enough for you. Your new target is to tell me when any of the work we do isn't sufficiently challenging; then I can make things more difficult for you.

7. Keep practising applying your target. I can see definite improvement in your work. More practice will take you closer to being successful. When you're practising, think about your target and what you're trying to achieve.

8. Take a look at the areas I've highlighted. These are the ones where you're furthest away from achieving your target. I'd like you to choose one of them to redo. Try and bring it closer into line with your target.

9. Compare this last piece of work with what you were doing a few months ago. You'll see how much you've developed by focussing on your targets. Keep this up with your new target.

10. Make a note of your target at the top of the page before you start your work. Go back to it while you are working to remind yourself of what you are trying to achieve.

11. You've been a bit inconsistent in applying your target. Sometimes you've got it spot on, sometimes you've gone a little bit off to one side. I'd like you to focus on consistently applying your target to every question.

12. I can see you've really got to grips with your target when it comes to practising long passing. Now I want to see you focussing on it in a game situation – with the added pressure of competition.

13. I'm going to increase the complexity of your original target. I'd like you to include at least three different elements in your routine, and I'd like to see a different transition between each one.

14. Now you've started to put your target into practice I'd like you to begin judging your own work before you hand it in. Identify where you've really hit your target and where you've fallen a bit short of what you want.

15. Choose a section of your work and redo it using your new target. When you've done, tell me why the new piece is different – and why it's better.

Knowledge

1. Include a greater level of detail in your work. Explain your ideas in full. I want to see that you know what you are talking about. If you're not sure, do some extra research.

2. Go into more depth when talking about the key points. For example, you could demonstrate what they mean in different situations and how they relate to one another.

3. Give examples to show that you know how the ideas connect to the real world. For example, you could talk about how electromagnetism is used in MRI machines.

4. I'd like to see you stay more focussed on the topic in future. I'm impressed at your wider knowledge, but try to make sure you bring this back to the topic and show how it relates.

5. Not all of the knowledge you've called on is relevant. Have a look at the questions I've highlighted. In these, you could have used more appropriate information. Revisit them and see if you can identify what you could have done differently.

6. You haven't used the key terms consistently all the way through. Have a look at how you've used the word 'democracy.' Rewrite the offending sentences and then tell me what the difference is.

7. More technical language would be good. This shows you have a broad knowledge of the topic. Try keeping the glossary to hand next time – use it to help you as you write your report.

8. I think you're relying on what you did last year. Next time, include more of what we've been learning this year. Don't worry if you make a mistake – you can learn from it.

9. The section I've highlighted contains knowledge which isn't appropriate for this question. While it's good stuff it doesn't add anything. See if you can think what would have been better to use, then call me over and we'll discuss it together.

10. Make connections between the different ideas you use. For example, you could show how migration has an impact on where and how governments spend their money.

11. Illustrate your ideas with examples and keywords. Use these to explain what your ideas mean and how they connect to the topic.

12. Some of your answers are too vague. We need to use knowledge really carefully in this unit. Rewrite your answers to questions 3, 8, 10 and 14. Make them more specific and precise.

13. You haven't used your knowledge to answer the question – you've answered a different one instead. Next time, start by making a note of what you know and then think about how it relates to the question. This will help you stay on track.

14. Your mock suggests you have some big gaps in your knowledge of forces and electricity. It's OK – that's what mocks are for! To find these things out. Your task is to go back and revisit those topics. Make flashcards and bring them in for me to look at with you.

15. I'd like you to practice half a dozen of these questions. On each one, think carefully about what knowledge is the most important to bring in, then make that the focus of your writing.

Editing/Rewriting

1. I've underlined a number of bits of your work that you could have edited yourself. Next time, remind yourself of this and make sure you edit in full before handing in.

2. Of the three sections of your leaflet, I think the third one is most in need of editing. It doesn't have the same level of detail as the other

sections. See if you can edit it to show me what you would do to make it better.

3. Overall, I think this is good but the story sags quite a bit in the middle compared to the start and end, which are nice and pacey. Choose one section from the middle and rewrite it so it is closer in feel to the start and end.

4. Your target is to explain each idea in full. This might mean sharing fewer ideas but going into detail about each one. Have a go at rewriting the first half of your essay in line with this target.

5. I'd like you to use an editing checklist before you hand your work in next time: spelling, punctuation, sense. First check your spellings, then check your punctuation, then check whether all your sentences make sense.

6. Try rewriting your answers using this set of questions: Am I answering the question? How am I deciding what information to include? Could I be more precise? Call me over and tell me about the differences after you've done it.

7. Choose three sentences you could edit. I'd like you to go for ones which aren't as clear as they could be. Write them underneath and then tell me why they are better.

8. You've used some of the keywords in different ways in different places. Have a look through and edit the ones you think aren't right. I'll take a look after you've done and we can discuss the changes.

9. Next time, I want to see a wider range of examples. This will show me that you are really thinking carefully about the topic. For now, choose one paragraph to rewrite and include a different example in it.

10. Your conclusion is flat. Look again at the rest of your essay. It maintains a critical edge throughout. Rewrite your conclusion so it contains a similar level of evaluative thinking.

11. Edit your code to remove some of the bugs I've highlighted. As you do, think about why your original code gave rise to the bugs – and be ready to tell me what you'll do differently next time.

12. You could definitely have said the same thing in fewer words. Edit your answer so it is simpler while retaining the same meaning.

13. There's not enough information in your story of what you did over the summer. I'd like you to rewrite the section about your holiday. Tell me more about what you did, where you went, what it felt like and what you enjoyed.

14. The language you've used makes it seem like you're writing for a friend. Imagine your audience was a group of professional scientists. Rewrite your findings and conclusion for them.

15. Clarity is key here. I want you to tell me what you think as clearly as possible. Go back and edit your thinking until it is crisper and clearer. Don't worry about making mistakes – they'll help you to get it right.

Effort

1. I think your effort dropped off as the task became more difficult. I'd like you to focus on sustaining your effort. Remind yourself to stay on track – even when the going gets tough.

2. Some of your answers are off topic. You should try to target your effort on the questions. As you write, ask yourself whether you're focussed on the question in hand. If not, bring yourself back on task.

3. Sometimes your effort is really good in lessons; sometimes you don't tend to focus as much. I'd like to see you putting in a good level of effort all the time. See if you can do that over the next couple of lessons.

4. When you hit a challenge, a good thing is to increase your effort levels rather than pulling back. The extra effort will help you to pick the challenge apart and work out how to beat it.

5. Target your effort on using more trial and error. If you're not sure how to do something, try going through a few different trials and see what happens. Use the information from your errors to change things around until you find what works.

6. I'd like you to be a better judge of your own effort. Identify a piece of work where you put in maximum effort and judge your future effort levels against this.

7. It's important to monitor your own effort in an activity like this. Next time, pay attention to how much you are putting in and identify where, when and why your effort levels drop.

8. Focussing on applying your target is a great way to get the most out of the effort you put in. When I give you your next target, I'd like you to write it at the top of the page and then concentrate on working towards it through the lesson.

9. Take a look at the two pieces of work I've highlighted. The first shows a really high level of effort; the second shows quite a low level of effort. Remind yourself what you did for the first one and try to do more of this next lesson.

10. If you get stuck, instead of giving up or waiting for the lesson to move on, tell me. That way I can help you to refocus your efforts and get more out of the learning.

11. Here are three questions you can use to assess your level of effort during a task: Is my mind wandering? Am I thinking about how I can be successful? Do I need any help or support so I can better focus my effort?

12. Have a look at the work you were producing and what you're doing now. You'll see the difference putting in a higher level of effort has brought about. Use this as motivation to keep doing the same thing.

13. You can improve your effort by breaking tasks down and focussing on one thing at a time. This will stop your mind getting overloaded.

14. A good way to control distractions is to make a list of the most common distractions you face and then remind yourself at the start of each lesson. That will help you to spot them and make the right choice.

15. One thing you might like to try next time is using bursts of effort. Instead of running round for the whole game, spend some time holding your position and then, when the time is right, use a burst of effort to affect the game.

Challenge

1. Challenge yourself to complete all the extension tasks. You are definitely capable of having a go at them and this will help you to really push your learning.

2. Identify a challenge you would like to take on over the next few weeks. Choose something connected to our topic and tell me why you think it will be a challenge and how you will tackle it.

3. Challenge yourself by attempting the harder problems first. Spend more time on these and then, if you have time left, use it to quickly work through the easier problems.

4. Tell me when the level of challenge is too low. If I don't know, I can't make the work more challenging for you. I want to make sure the learning is pushing you to reach your potential!

5. If you're sometimes getting stuck, this is usually a sign that the level of challenge is about right. Next time you get stuck, let me know and we'll discuss what's happened, why it's a challenge and how to get past it.

6. I'd like you to see challenges as a positive thing. Next time you find yourself facing a challenge, ask yourself what you might learn from it and remind yourself that trying different strategies is always an option.

7. Make a list of the different strategies you can use when faced with a challenge. Show me the list and we'll talk it through. You can then use this when you next face a challenge.

8. Use trial and error the next time you get stuck. See if you can try different ways of aiming to solve the problem. Watch what happens and keep adjusting things until you get it right.

9. Your target is to seek out challenges in every lesson. This could mean working hard to get onto the extension or asking me to make the work more difficult for you. It's about you taking ownership of the level of challenge.

10. I want you to make at least two mistakes, or get stuck once, every lesson. This will show me that you are stretching yourself and that your

thinking is being challenged. If you get halfway through the lesson and haven't made a mistake or become stuck, let me know.

11. Pick a section of the work I've marked and tell me how we could increase the level of challenge. Then, try redoing that section so it fits in with this new standard.

12. I'd like to see more evaluation in your answers. Tell me what's good and what's bad; what works and what doesn't. This will show me you're really challenging yourself to think critically.

13. Being original is a challenge – and I'd like you to embrace it. Instead of mimicking the work we've studied, use it as a starting point to think of your own ideas.

14. You can challenge yourself by reading more widely. Take a look at the list of books I've written out. We won't look at these in class, but I think you'll really benefit from reading some. Pick one to get you started.

15. I think you've got to grips with serving. Now I want to see you mastering the technique by increasing the accuracy of your serves. Challenge yourself by practising serves to specific areas of the court.

Strengths

1. Play to your strengths more often. You're really good when speaking in debates, so try talking your ideas through before you start writing. This will make it easier to say what you want to say in your essays.

2. Keep working on your understanding of quantum mechanics. I'm really impressed at how this has developed over the last couple of weeks. Keep plugging away at it and you'll develop an even better understanding.

3. Don't rest on your laurels. It's tempting to sit back when you've achieved such a high score. I'd like you to think about how you could push your strengths further. Let me know what I can do to help.

4. Try using your strengths in listening to help improve your speaking. Listen carefully to how some professionals speakers speak on YouTube and identify what you could borrow from them.

5. Your ability to describe the key ideas is excellent – I can see this from your work. Now I'd like you to be more nuanced in your descriptions. Think about how you can bring shades of grey into them.

6. You're really strong at answering the 6-mark questions. Take the method you use and apply it to the 12-mark questions. You might need to make some tweaks but I think this will help you to develop.

7. Tell me why this piece of work is good. I want to see that you understand why it is good and what strengths you have used to make it good. Then, tell me how you can use these same strengths in the future.

8. I can see your strong imagination coming through in the beginning of your story, but not so much at the end. I'd like you to concentrate on using this strength all the way through. Try reminding yourself of it after every few paragraphs you write.

9. I don't think we saw the best of your dribbling today. You went back to the old habit of trying to go past one player too many. Focus on combining your strength in dribbling with making sure you get a good final ball.

10. Take a look at your last piece of work and the one I've just marked. Can you see the difference? I think you made your last target into a strength, but then forgot about it in the most recent work. Next time, focus on getting yourself back up to that standard.

11. I'd like you to start identifying the strengths in your work before handing it in. We can then see if we both agree. This will help you to develop a better understanding of where you are at and how you are developing.

12. Try changing your approach next time round. I know you've become really skilled at developing routines in this style, but now I'd like you to start developing strengths in other areas as well.

13. Challenge yourself to keep improving your strengths. For example, you could try writing a more complex melody or come up with an original chord progression.

14. Build on your existing strengths by using your knowledge of the local area to bring more detail and information into your report. Think about some of the extra things you could include.

15. Make a list of your strengths and then show me where each of these comes into play in your next piece of work. Call me over while you're working and talk me through some of the things you notice.

Chapter Eleven – Conclusion and Select Bibliography

Feedback and marking are an essential feature of every teacher's work. Feedback gives access to your expertise. It is the way in which you help learners understand what they are doing well and what they can improve. Without feedback, the classroom is a sparser place and learning suffers. Marking allows you to elicit rich information about students' knowledge, understanding and progress. You can use this information to underpin the judgements you make and the feedback you give.

You should never underestimate the scope of your expertise and the importance of leading the learning in your classroom. Students are novices. They are there to learn and develop. You are highly skilled, knowledgeable and well-informed. This combination makes you a teacher and distinguishes you from your students. It is on this accumulated expertise that you call when you mark student work and give feedback. Throughout the year, you are consistently giving students access to your expertise, so that they might benefit from this and, with effort and practice, make it their own.

Feedback and marking are all well and good, but their positive impacts will likely be lost if learners do not have time in which to act on the information they receive from you. Without dedicated time in which to reflect on targets, discuss them with peers and attempt to implement them, learners will invariably find themselves caught up in the flow of content characterising the school day. Targets will be lost as a result.

There are many ways in which you can make sure that time is available. The key is to find a way that works for you and your learners. By making use of regular verbal feedback during tasks and activities you will also give learners plenty of opportunities to take advantage of your expertise in the moment.

This book contains a wide range of strategies and techniques you can employ to improve and develop your feedback and marking. There is too much to do at once. Better instead to select a few ideas that really chime with you and how you teach. Use these as they are presented or adapt them to fit your style. Persist with them over the course of a few months and analyse the effect they have on learning, motivation and progress. Then make a decision whether to persist with them, modify them or try something else. In other words, don't be afraid to engage in some trial and error to find what works best for you.

Ultimately, there are many ways in which feedback and marking can be made effective. But the central themes of this book will always ring true: give access to your expertise, give time in which students can act on this, support learners to do this effectively, and use marking as a way to elicit rich information about where your learners are at. Keeping these themes in mind will help you to be successful and should help you to raise achievement and have a sustained positive impact on your students and their learning. And in that endeavour I wish you luck.

Select Bibliography

Paul Black et al (2003), *Assessment for Learning: Putting it Into Practice*

Shirley Clarke (2014), *Outstanding Formative Assessment*

Carol Dweck (2000), *Self-Theories: Their Role in Motivation, Personality and Development*

John Hattie (2008), *Visible Learning*

John Hattie (2012), *Visible Learning for Teachers*

Steve Higgins, Dimitra Kokotsaki and Robert Coe (2012), *The Education Endowment Foundation Teaching and Learning Toolkit*

Ian Smith (2014), *Assessment for Learning Pocketbook*

Isabella Wallace and Leah Kirkman (eds) (2017), *Best of the Best: Feedback*

Dylan Wiliam and Paul Black (1990)), *Inside the Black Box*

Dylan Wiliam (2011), *Embedded Formative Assessment*

Printed in Great Britain
by Amazon